WHEN THE THUNDERS SPEAK

Unmasking the 666

WHEN THE THUNDERS SPEAK

Unmasking the 666

MELVIN E. PAREDES-FORZANI

Copyright © 2021 Melvin Ernesto Paredes Forzani
All rights reserved.

No part of this book may be reproduced in any form or by any means—electronic, mechanical, photocopying, recording, scanning, or otherwise—without the express written permission of the author.

ISBN 978-1-7778731-0-3

DEDICATION

To those who were murdered for defending the truth.

And [he] cried with a loud voice as a lion roars. And when he cried, the seven thunders uttered their own voices.

—Revelation 10:3 (Darby Translation)

CONTENTS

	PREFACE	xi
1.	ENCODED MESSAGE	1
	The mysterious letter	1
	Protecting the doctrine	4
	From Patmos to the Canon	7
2.	THE SEVEN SPIRITS OF GOD	11
	Unblemished	12
	To the seven assemblies	14
	The perfect harmony of a design	19
3.	THE HERD, THE SOCIETY	23
	Running without direction	23
	The dubious decency of the collective mind	27
	Restoring discernment	31
4.	SEALED BOOK	37
	The great expectation	37
	Coming out of the shadows	40
	Worthy to open the scroll	42
5.	HORSEMEN OF CANAAN	45
	Faithful and True	46
	Conflict between two kingdoms	48
	The temple's scale	49
	The first destruction	51
6.	TRUE PROPHETS	55
	Blood of prophets	55
	Sharper than any two-edged sword	59
	The fig tree is shaken	63
	A sowing field	67
7.	LOCUSTS DOMINION	69
	Locusts over the earth	69
	Torment men five months	75
	The appearance of the locusts	79
	Breastplates of fire, jacinth and sulfur	86

- **8. JESUS AGAINST THE FIG TREE** 93
  - The fruitless temple 93
  - Seal the things spoken 96
  - Two witnesses 99
  - With the moon under her feet 106
  - The red dragon 108
  - A beast with authority for 42 months 111
- **9. THE FALSE PROPHET** 115
  - The mystery of the false prophet 115
  - Counting the number of the beast 116
  - The most reliable Greek Pentateuch 118
  - Exposing the identity of the false prophet 119
  - The accuser of our brothers 130
  - Two paths leading in opposite directions 132
- **10. RETAKING THE PATH** 141
  - What is truth? 141
  - The purpose of creation 142
  - The distorter 143
  - Corruption of the mind 146
  - Two dictators, lust and gluttony 152
  - Comfortable dungeon of mammon 160
  - The spirit begins where tradition ends 161
  - ABOUT THE AUTHOR 167

PREFACE

The answer to an ancient riddle is given within these words, a mystery that has been the source of great perplexity for almost two thousand years: the exact identification of the controversial figure known as the beast and the meaning behind its infamous number 666. But even more shocking is discovering that this figure has already influenced the lives of countless people, among whom the majority of our readers are included, even if they are not willing to admit it. Hence the importance of revealing the true meaning of the Book of Revelation, for although the letter was written about two millennia ago, its message continues to be relevant for those who are seeking understanding. Despite how complex its words appear to be at first glance, Revelation was neither written to confuse nor to entertain but to advise and vindicate.

The mysterious book has drawn so much curiosity that throughout much of history numerous interpretations have been written about its meaning. The different interpretations range from the complex to the sensationalist, from beliefs about the future to theories about past events, but they were nothing more than assumptions that wilt in the midst of doubt. However, when the evidence presented becomes so overwhelming that it cannot be attributed to simple coincidence, interpretations come to an end, and certainty clears the way. Within the Book of Revelation, there are enough elements to arrive at a convincing conclusion about the letter's message, but only by understanding the true meaning behind the number 666 can all doubt be dissipated, and everything becomes clear once and for all.

Although many clues are given throughout the writing to describe the beast, the key piece that categorically confirms its identity is the infamous number of its name, 666. Such a meaning is conclusive evidence because, as it will be shown later, it is simple to understand and verify, and, at the same time, it is impossible for another figure to meet that condition. Moreover, as if that were not enough, that character also meets all the other elements that the author of Revelation uses to describe the beast.

It is very easy to misinterpret the writing because of its strange analogies and peculiar words, but understanding the true meaning of the letter will prove that the author of Revelation never intended to create more confusion; on the contrary, he was trying to clarify a fundamental issue that was extremely dangerous to deal with openly; hence, he was forced to disguise his words so that the letter could not be understood by the enemies of the truth and would be able to reach its destination without being destroyed or altered. In order to avoid the misunderstandings that could arise among the people to whom the letter was addressed, the author of Revelation determined that he needed to leave such a definitive clue that there would be no doubt about the true identity of the false prophet, a clue that after being discovered would serve to provide the valuable certainty that is demanded by the skeptics, sought by the prudent and much needed by the deceived.

Revelation was not written by a delirious man, much less by a swindler, but by a brilliant mind and a concerned soul that tried to protect and vindicate valuable teachings that were being despised and, to some extent, altered by the aberrations of man. Behind the writing, there is a very noble and well-founded intention, and as we advance in the understanding of its mysterious words, it will be

PREFACE

demonstrated that the ancient letter carries a specific and immensely useful message for humanity.

Any honest writing has the ultimate goal of, sooner or later, making its message comprehensible for the intended readers, and the Book of Revelation was no exception. Revelation rescues a doctrine that initially was capable of attaining the absolute reformation of its followers and the total eradication of ignorance, but the process had stalled due to the great deception of the beast, which with great signs and authority has been persuading men to follow most of its instructions up to this day.

For that reason, the meaning of the ancient writing continues to have great significance; through its words, the false prophet is stripped naked, leaving him uncovered before all, with the purpose of bringing understanding so that men become able to abandon those deceitful teachings that were full of stains and take on a journey to perfect their ways. Thus, we are convinced that uncovering the true message of the Book of Revelation is of vital importance for the progress of mankind, although at the beginning it will cause many controversies that would appear to be counterproductive. But time and reflection will prove that the truth was never meant to remain hidden. A very wise man once said to us:

> *Therefore, don't be afraid of them, for there is nothing covered that will not be revealed; and hidden that will not be known. What I tell you in the darkness, speak in the light; and what you hear whispered in the ear, proclaim on the housetops. (Matthew 10:26-27 DBY)*

Clarity along the way is what leads to understanding, while uncertainty begets a hesitant soul that is always fearful of taking a step forward.

Due to the great controversy that will arise from the shocking message, it would be very irresponsible if we reveal the identity of the mysterious false prophet without first providing the means to understand how this can be used to straighten our ways. First and foremost, it is necessary to gradually strengthen the reader's bowels so that he can digest the food that must be eaten; if he does not develop the capacity to assimilate it in the proper manner, such food could cause more harm than good. Before knowing the true meaning of Revelation, the reader should rise above the conflicts and gossip that could be caused by the controversial writing, and he should not try to manipulate the message with the intention of using the unveiling of the identity of the false prophet as an excuse to discard all the other teachings that indeed are true and just.

Revealing the meaning behind the number 666 without first providing a good foundation is the same as rescuing a child from the hands of his abductor and then leaving the little child alone in the middle of an immense forest. Before unveiling the message, it is crucial to provide the tools so that man may continue the journey towards the truth on his own. The chapters of this book that are not directly related to Revelation were not written to decorate this work but to cleanse the mind and strengthen the soul of the reader so that he is able to use the shocking message to move forward.

Because of the controversial message of the Book of Revelation, one might think that these words are meant to overturn the good traditions of men; yet, the ultimate purpose behind this work is not to destroy but to build. However, you cannot build a new and lasting house when the land is occupied by an old one with a poorly built foundation.

Since no one would dare to destroy their own house without first knowing how to build a new one, it becomes critical to reflect on certain teachings that were given to us around two thousand years ago in order to gain the necessary knowledge to build the new home with a truly solid foundation.

In the process, many will be afraid of being left homeless and will find it difficult to destroy that old house; nevertheless, be brave,

PREFACE

or at least curious, and do not forget that the unknown seems unpleasant or even frightening at first, but knowledge always brings us closer to reality and creates better conditions for those who enjoy the truth.

Reluctance to change is what has always sustained ignorance. Everyone wants to find the true meaning of life, but few are willing to give up their old habits and customs that distort their perception. A man who is not willing to question his own behavior will never recognize the need for change, so his quest for truth is nothing more than entertainment and vanity. If you really want to see beyond what your eyes allow you to see, then act accordingly.

I

ENCODED MESSAGE

The mysterious letter

"And when the seven thunders spoke, I was about to write: and I heard a voice out of the heaven saying, Seal the things which the seven thunders have spoken, and write them not" (Revelation 10:4 Darby Translation). In this manner, the message of the Book of Revelation was sealed for almost two thousand years, but it was never meant to remain hidden for so long; its true meaning was always out in the open, and perhaps some were able to understand it. Perhaps the circumstances forced them to keep it hidden, and, if that was the case, after long-lasting persecutions, those few men and women probably disappeared with the passage of time without being able to make known the true meaning of the writing.

It is not possible to determine if anyone from the distant past was able to decode the true meaning of the writing because if such a person ever existed, the conditions of his time would never have allowed him to come out publicly. But what is now certain is that the circumstances have changed, and today the message can be revealed to all of humanity without the fear of having the writing being destroyed by anyone. It has become impossible to suppress the dissemination of knowledge, not only because of freedom of speech but also due to advancements in technology. Now the conditions are in place to unveil the mystery of the letter and culminate the noble task that the author of Revelation set out to accomplish.

For about two thousand years, the Book of Revelation has remained a great mystery that has perplexed anyone who has read it. Examined and admired by many but understood by few, its true meaning, which continues to be important—even after two millennia—, will impact you and change the way you see the world, it will challenge your beliefs and make you reflect on your habits. If you are humble enough to welcome the discernment that the ancient writing offers you, you will find a great truth that had been buried by the ignorance of man.

Revelation is not just a book. The brilliant way with which its author John hides the powerful message within its lines proves that the writing is a magnificent intellectual work; while the depth of the message reveals a discernment that is inspired by the type of wisdom that cannot be found in the ordinary world. The Book of Revelation is much more than a simple narrative; it is an instruction and an exhaustive explanation of the truth, with the objective of empowering human beings to become what they were predestined to be.

The ancient letter is full of concealed messages. For instance, close to the end, John writes, "And I saw a new heaven and a new earth; for the first heaven and the first earth had passed away, and the sea exists no more" (Revelation 21:1), at first glance, these lines seem to be self-explanatory, but its true meaning is deeper than what can be seen on the surface. That and many other hidden messages will become clear as we move forward, searching for the truth. It will also become even more evident why the author of the letter had to encode the message.

Among the mysterious remarks of the writing is the reference to the infamous 666, a number that, in itself alone, is enough to reveal the identity of the false prophet—also known as the beast—in a definitive way, without requiring complex equations or exuberant assumptions. Yet, we need spiritual maturity in order to understand the implications as well as a sincere humility to accept that the vast majority of men, even those who consider themselves to be just and wise, have not only been persuaded by this figure, but they are also so attached to him that even after witnessing the light, they prefer to remain in the dark by his side.

Unmasking that great obstacle that has seized our discernment is one of the main purposes of the Book of Revelation. That is why the book focuses on the figure of the beast and its number 666—commonly known as the number of the antichrist—, who, by the great signs that he is able to do, persuades men to be his followers.

Many believe that this character was a Roman emperor who brutally persecuted Christians. Others argue that he was a Pontifex Maximus of the Catholic Church, and others think that it refers to a geopolitical leader who has not arrived yet. However, they are all aiming at the wrong target. In fact, the bull's eye has always been on our own foreheads; for that reason, it has been impossible to identify it.

Only by observing ourselves and our traditions in the mirror of introspection can we see the clues that will help us find the truth in order to discover the identity of the beast.

It may be hard to believe, but the figure behind the 666 has already influenced the lives of billions of people and most likely has also persuaded you to become his follower. He is not an emperor, but his reach has gone further than any empire, and his influence has not been matched by any political or religious leader. If the message of Revelation is not revealed, the power of persuasion of the beast will continue to lead men to a dark abyss of ignorance.

The words of the Book of Revelation are often taken out of context and seen with a sense of sensationalism. The reader often finds it hard to understand that the letter is encoded in more ways than we could imagine. Most readers get excited by the wonders narrated in the final victory without ever realizing that they are the faithful followers of the beast.

Protecting the doctrine

Through analogies and symbolism, the writing vindicates teachings that were transmitted from generation to generation and that were perfected with the words of Jesus. When his words were heard by men who were willing to put their minds in order, they were enough to pull them out of the ignorance in which they were submerged. His teachings brought understanding once and for all, not partially, and eliminated all confusion about the ways of man in relation to the truth.

However, at the time, a large obstacle prevented such teachings from being transmitted openly and in its purest form. Sadly, even to this day, the same obstacle continues to persuade us to cover our ears and does not allow us to understand what Jesus was trying to tell us. This great obstacle, the mountain that needs to be thrown into the sea, has constrained man's vision by deceiving him and has cut short an admirable work that must be resumed as soon as possible.

Since long ago, inspired men sought to change the corrupted state of humanity, but their efforts were constantly thwarted by the figure behind the 666 and everything that it represented and still represents. For this reason, the reformation of man has been halted; here lies the importance of writing this book, for man has been living a lie thinking that he had reached his spiritual goal, when in fact he stopped halfway.

Truth has been abducted by deception. After realizing that the destruction of documents related to the teachings of Jesus could not make him disappear, deception was used to blur the truth with a watered-down version of it. Only that which is easy to tolerate is

ENCODED MESSAGE

accepted by the doctrines of the world, while everything that opposes their habits and customs is discarded without even being analyzed. We all have wronged by altering the truth for the sake of our own convenience; if we do not have the means to change it on a piece of paper, then we change it in our own personal misinterpretations. Instead of straightening up himself so that his body fits the teaching, man is always eager to alter any teaching so that it can fit his deformed body.

The true teachings of Jesus were repudiated by the vast majority, who did not understand his words and saw them as an affront to their way of thinking. Even today, things have not changed much, as people love to mention the name Jesus but despise his words and never bother to dig deeper into his teachings. We have taken teachings that were pure and have covered them in dirt with our weaknesses and false perception. Teachings that showed people how to reform themselves completely, in a tangible manner, later became a doctrine that settled for accepting the weaknesses of men as a permanent condition, arguing that the only thing that is necessary to achieve the ultimate goal of creation was to shed the innocent blood of Jesus.

Seeing how time after time ancient teachings were being altered caused great disappointment among those who were trying to protect the truth. On that account, the author of Revelation decided to write a clear warning in the last words of his letter to prevent it from being altered. In that way, Revelation becomes the only writing of the biblical canon that explicitly warns that nothing should be added or removed; John makes this precise clarification because he is aware that many of the earlier writings had already been modified, and he needed to ensure that this common practice was not going to be repeated in this case. But most importantly, Revelation is also the only book of the biblical canon that is encoded from beginning to end. For that reason, the letter is the least altered book of the Bible since men, in addition to being threatened by the author's warning, were greatly perplexed by the degree of complexity of the book. In this manner, the author manages to keep the message intact, avoiding the usual alterations that are made by men.

It is dishonest to say that all the books of the Bible are intact and that they were able to survive all the atrocities that occurred during the persecutions without having been modified in any way. Many people argue that the scriptures could not have been altered because God is all-powerful, but they ignore the fact that the greatness of creation and existence rests upon the free will of us all, who in many instances managed to establish our crooked ways over those of the Creator. Yet, many people still claim that nothing has been added or removed from the scriptures. Perhaps they say so because it is very easy to affirm such a thing from the comfort of our lives, but the brave men and women who defended the truth and were victims of great atrocities would say that if the scriptures were impossible to adulterate, they would not have felt the need to risk their lives and go through so much hardship to protect those writings.

In fact, the followers of truth were given only two choices, and neither was favorable: one option was to surrender and hand over all the writings in their possession to be immediately destroyed, and even doing so did not guarantee that torture was going to be avoided; and the other option was to remain silent and be martyred, which could also mean the loss of any writing when no one else knew its whereabouts, not even those for whom it was intended.

Either option led to very unfortunate outcomes, and the writings that were too hot to handle most likely were lost or altered, except one, which by being disguised managed to survive without modifications; yes indeed, that is the letter of Revelation, which is at the very end of that collection of books that we all know as the Bible.

From Patmos to the Canon

The Book of Revelation passed its first test when it was able to make it out of the island of Patmos intact with a message as risky as the one it was carrying, and it passed its second test when, against all odds, it was included in the official list of books recognized by the main churches of antiquity, being part of what later would be known as the biblical canon. But its journey to the place where it is now was not easy. Before, and even after, being declared canonical, Revelation was criticized by those people who could not understand the purpose of the book, while the clergymen who favored its inclusion, despite being very literate, understood only a fraction of its content; thus, the defense of the writing was always at a disadvantage due to its complexity.

In spite of that, the moral integrity of the book, along with other forces that we could only describe as divine providence, carried it along so that it would survive and take its rightful place, avoiding what had happened to other valuable documents that were destroyed during the persecutions of the first Christians, whose writings contained strong words that men did not want to hear. Ignorance is always comfortable for those who have become accustomed to the darkness, just like the man who desires to continue sleeping hates the light. The brighter the light emanating from a teaching, the more enraged will be those who are in a deep sleep. For that simple reason, the early followers of Jesus were threatened and tortured until they were forced to confess the location of their writings.

Although the Book of Revelation was never understood in its entirety, it had been cited since the second century by emblematic figures of Christianity of the time, such as Justin Martyr, Irenaeus of Lyons, Tertullian, and Clement of Alexandria; by the third century, it was being accepted by the majority of Christians throughout the Roman Empire. However, despite its popularity, the process for its official acceptance was slow and caused more friction than other writings, as it was expected. By the middle of the first millennium, it had already been included in important compilations, such as Codex Sinaiticus, Codex Alexandrinus and the one from the Council of Carthage in the year 397.

The book is a genuine source of wisdom not because a group of mortal men so decided, but because when it is read carefully, with good discernment and without any sensationalism, it becomes clear that the letter has no stains in its arguments and can edify greatly; and if the reader, with a sincere heart, were to endeavor to understand the true meaning of Revelation, after finally finding it, he would have no other choice but to regard the writing as a work worthy of admiration in every sense, especially the spiritual.

As for the date of the writing, it is futile to begin a debate about the very specific period in which it was written or who wrote it; at this point, we will only say that it was written between 60-100 C.E. This period provides a range that covers the various hypotheses concerning its origins and avoids long debates so that we can focus on what is important. Our sight must be set on the message, which is extremely critical and edifying.

Like those men who more than 500 years before him began to cry out for the truth to be known, John never had the opportunity to enjoy what in this era is known as freedom of speech, much less was he able to experience religious freedom, which today is a basic right in most civilized countries. During those times, life was risky for every man who felt the need to instruct with the truth, opposing head-on the thoughts and behavior of the majority. The only way to transmit their message in public was by suffering the consequences of being declared enemies of the people as well as enemies of the god they supposedly offended.

ENCODED MESSAGE

Hiding his message using a myriad of symbolisms was necessary for John. It was a matter of life and death. Had the message been discovered by the wrong people, it would have been condemned as a crime and would never have reached its intended recipients, let alone making it to the biblical canon. Destruction would have been the fate for both John and his message; John would have ended up on a cross or being stoned to death under the charge of blasphemy, and—what he perhaps considered even more tragic—his letter would have been burned without us ever knowing about it.

However, how wonderful and mysterious is this life that the writing not only managed to survive without having experienced major alterations, but it also became part of the biblical canon against all odds. Moreover, today, after almost two thousand years, we live in times in which the true message can be revealed without censorship and may be shared with the entire world at almost the speed of light. In this modern age, information can no longer be suppressed by anything or anyone. It can no longer be altered or destroyed. The hour has come to continue the reformation of man and at the same time give their reward to the righteous people who were mocked and scorned and, on many occasions, even murdered.

Writing from a remote place known as the island of Patmos, the author of Revelation was able to provoke the interest of numerous cultures, generation after generation, without losing strength or relevance. And, without getting ahead of ourselves, more than achieving its inclusion in the biblical canon, the writing has the power to redefine the way we see the compendium of books to which it belongs.

2

THE SEVEN SPIRITS OF GOD

The spirit is a servant of the truth, not a slave of traditions. Certainly, unveiling the mystery behind the 666, besides the great controversy that it could create if it is not approached with a sufficient degree of maturity, has the potential to end a whole system of beliefs that has come to govern our behavior; hence, it could be dangerous and very frustrating for the minds of those men whose faith is based on traditions rather than principles, on the commandments of men rather than on the truth from the conscience. There are revelations that could create storms capable of tearing down our current beliefs, but that is not necessarily a bad thing if we are willing to take the next step forward in understanding.

Before hastening to reveal a message that has been hidden for about two thousand years, it would be wise to take a little more time to lay the foundations to strengthen the spirit as well as our discernment. It is necessary to learn from the teachings of early Christianity, which was conceived without aberrations or distortions; it was unblemished.

WHEN THE THUNDERS SPEAK

Unblemished

"And to the angel of the assembly in Sardis write: These things saith he that has the seven Spirits of God, and the seven stars" (Revelation 3:1).

The message of Revelation must be approached from the perspective of the early Christians who were entrusted with a very particular teaching embodied in the words of Jesus, whose impeccable example is illustrated by describing him as the one who possesses the seven Spirits of God. The early Christians did not aspire to little; they were well aware that the teachings of Jesus were capable of reforming the souls of men to their fullness, never partially; that is, they continuously aimed for perfection on values such as humility, meekness, self-control and loving the neighbor.

The early followers of Jesus were not trying to create a simple religion or sect like the many others that already existed at that time. They were pursuing the concept of achieving a tangible transformation that would lead them to know the reality of their own existence. They knew that the doctrines that preceded Jesus always led to indifference and intolerance; one single flaw in such doctrines was enough to eventually drown any man in confusion. Instead, early Christians recognized as flawless the truth behind the teachings of Jesus, who showed them the importance of loving even their enemies, not desiring material wealth, serving others and not allowing illusory pleasures to reign over their minds.

It is important to delve into the minds of the early followers of Jesus because their way of seeing life allowed them to easily differentiate between false prophets and true messengers; between idolatrous rituals and sincere contemplation; between the abuse of power and the discipline that arises from real understanding. It is never profitable to cling to traditions when they are detrimental to the truth.

THE SEVEN SPIRITS OF GOD

They knew that a true messenger does not flaunt his imperfections as if they were virtues; he does not seek to destroy souls with the excuse of pleasing God, nor does he try to legitimize man's weaknesses by promoting ways of violence, indifference and greed, perpetuating darkness by alleging that we have been justified.

We should not expect to keep on living with the same weaknesses for the rest of our lives, eternally immersed in a state of ignorance that just hopes to be forgiven. Forgiveness by itself does not remove the blindfold from the one who is forgiven; it is the willingness to seize the opportunity to start over from another perspective that in fact heals the sight. What good is it to be forgiven if there is no intention to change our ways? Being aware of this, the early followers of Jesus knew that the only way towards true understanding was by overcoming all the weaknesses that cloud our vision.

But those first Christians were nothing like the groups of people that follow a set of superficial rules without even knowing what spiritual benefit they could derive from those instructions, which they obey blindly for the sole purpose of receiving a reward in return. Fanatics are lovers of intolerance and vanity, an attitude that was condemned by the words of Jesus, whose teachings define such behavior as superficial and hypocritical. Rather, early Christians lived according to a group of virtues and values that were a reflection of the beauty of the spirit and the objectivity of reality. In their quest for the truth, they valued all qualities equally, from the simplicity of service and humbleness to the power of self-control and faith.

As long as there is a flaw in a man's character, he must continue to strengthen himself until all faculties of the spirit are able to genuinely spring forth, without hypocrisy, as his new nature. Only in that manner will man be able to see the world for what it really is and recognize the true fruit of Jesus' teachings; for this reason, while addressing the behavior of the seven assemblies of Asia Minor, Jesus insists on not overlooking any of the weaknesses of man.

To the seven assemblies

There is a section in the Book of Revelation that is often ignored. Nevertheless, it is crucial not only to understand the writing but also to come out of the spiritual stagnation in which we find ourselves. In the message that Jesus sends to the seven assemblies of Asia Minor, he identifies the weaknesses of the members of each assembly and also recognizes the virtues they possess. His intention is to make clear that they should not stop until they have overcome all of their weaknesses, with no exception, because the truth is unblemished, and the soul is not to be reformed partially.

To illustrate the concept, it is convenient to use the example of the assembly of Thyatira, which seems to have the most attributes according to Jesus' words when he says:

> *I know thy works, and love, and faith, and service, and thine endurance, and thy last works to be more than the first. But I have against thee that thou permittest the woman Jezebel, she who calls herself prophetess, and she teaches and leads astray my servants to commit fornication and eat of idol sacrifices. (Revelation 2:19-20)*

All the virtues cited above, in addition to self-control, which is mentioned as a reproach because it is the only one they are still lacking, are real and tangible qualities that bring clarity to men's vision and not simply a group of trivial or absurd laws such as the ones obeyed by those who love false doctrines. These virtues are essential tools needed to develop the spirit of men through the understanding of reality. They are not empty laws to be obeyed blindly with the intention of receiving a prize after death; on the contrary, they are attributes that, when perfected, are capable of transforming a man's life while he is still on earth. One of the most valuable rewards given to man is his own reformation since his true existence begins and is sustained with every step he takes toward discovering a fascinating reality which was unknown to him before. With so much yet to see, there is no better trophy than removing the blindfold.

While carnal weaknesses cloud the vision by making us live in a fantasy where only the self exists, spiritual qualities eliminate everything that distorts man's perception. Just by developing certain virtues is man able to end his ignorance and achieve the objectivity necessary to realize his own existence, which comes to life when he eradicates selfishness along with its great distorters of reality: fear, vanity, anger and the weaknesses of the flesh. This is why it is important for the author of the Book of Revelation to recognize the attributes of the members of the assemblies while at the same time encouraging them to overcome each of their remaining weaknesses.

In the case of Thyatira, its members perfected their works, love, service, faith, patience—endurance—and that their last works are more than the first, but some of them still lacked self-control since they had been persuaded to "commit sexual immorality, and to eat things sacrificed to idols." As for those who did not follow such behavior, showing, in that sense, self-control besides the other six virtues that had been mastered, Jesus tells them: "I am not putting any other burden on you" (Revelation 2:24).

Yet, those virtues should not be confused with their diffused mundane reflections that can be seen, to some extent, in the ordinary behavior of men, such as the faith of a scientist in his theory, the patience of a passionate teacher or the unconditional love of a mother. These examples are just little fragments of the reality enclosed by those qualities, whose true proportions can only be understood from an entirely different angle than the one from our worldly and distorted perception. When man's peace of mind becomes so stable that it would be almost impossible to frustrate, only then will he have attained patience and endurance; when a mother and father become capable of loving a stranger with the same intensity with which they love their child, only then will they be able to know the true meaning of charity; and when man's awareness becomes more reliable than simple perception, at last will he have experienced true faith.

It is important to remember that virtuous faith in no way resembles blind faith. The latter is born of ignorance and is nothing more than a "lack of faith" in self-discernment, which is a fundamental gift conferred on us that must always be put to use. When blind faith is the argument used to defend a questionable behavior, it is an insult to everyone's innate wisdom and capacity to hear for themselves the voice of that which created them. There are those who commit violence by arguing that they do so because of their great faith, but they forget that it is better to have faith in mercy and forgiveness than in wickedness dictated by ink and paper. Whoever trusts in another man more than in his own ability to discern has surrendered to a stranger his valuable conscience, without which man is but a mere machine that eats, sleeps and breathes. Virtuous faith would never give rise to atrocities, for by sustaining itself in reflection, it becomes the fuel that leads man to continually improve his ways with determination, detaching himself from the ambiguity that comes from ignorance while holding on to the certainty that comes from understanding.

Another attribute that is mentioned concerning the members of Thyatira is the often-underestimated virtue of service, a faculty that is just as important as the rest since by learning humility and embracing simplicity, man is able to overcome the illusions of vanity and pride that permanently undermine his ability to live the detached life that is needed for the spirit to spring forth. Very often it is simple vanity, not laziness, that makes people love being served while despising serving others, because their pride cannot bear to see itself in situations in which people might perceive them as weak or insignificant, without ever realizing that insignificant is he whose life is of no use to others. A true leader is not someone who gives orders but someone whose drive to serve others makes him a good example to follow. Those who serve are always better apt to be leaders than those who want to be served.

Man can hardly walk forward when he is dragging all the heavy burdens that the ego has persuaded him to take on his journey, but simplicity throws away all the unnecessary baggage so that his soul can move freely. Reality can only be seen through simplicity, while vanity can only see itself.

When writing about the assembly of Thyatira, the author of Revelation also states that their "last works are more than the first," alluding to the principle of continuous improvement. One of man's most grave errors is believing that he has at last reached understanding. In such cases, he ends up being worse off than when he started because now he becomes stuck indefinitely by thinking that there is nothing else to strengthen. He who humbly acknowledges all of his weaknesses and is continually seeking ways to eradicate them is closer to the truth than the illustrious man who is satisfied with his present condition. There are no limits to the perfecting of the soul; there will always be something new to learn or refine. Stagnation is for those who think that reality is ruled by the flesh.

The great importance of the remaining virtues of love, works and patience is evident, and we do not need to elaborate on them. Regardless of all the virtues found within Thyatira, their only flaw is not overlooked: the weakness of the flesh, which is a stumbling block for the assembly of Pergamum as well. Even after developing six spiritual qualities, the members of Thyatira are still being warned against fornication and eating things sacrificed to idols. Due to the deceptive nature of carnal weaknesses, the lack of self-control has become the stumbling block for those who are just a few steps away from knowing the truth, for reality is still being distorted by their own infirmities. When self-control is lacking, desires become necessities, and reality has to be sold to afford them.

Because of its harmless appearance, the weakness of the flesh has become the most underestimated enemy by the majority of men. Very often the lack of self-control is established as the norm and seen as a blessing. People try to justify what is certainly self-indulgence, arguing that it is being done in moderation; however, what selfishness sees as moderation is in reality an exaggeration for those who truly have to pay for the cost of such addictions. On other occasions, the same people who in public condemn reprehensible actions, in the privacy of their minds they welcome worse thoughts and believe that they are not at fault if the action does not take place, never noticing that the greatest harm that is caused by the lack of self-control occurs precisely within the mind, not on the outside.

Controlling our instincts is just the beginning in the pursuit of the truth, which continues with the mastering of our thoughts and ends only when man's preferences are transformed to the point where his perception of reality ceases to be a simple interpretation based on his weaknesses; so that hypocrisy is no longer part of him and his mind is not in conflict with itself. True self-control develops with reflection, practice and patience and does not finish its work until man loves the truth, enjoys the equanimity of his actions and is not ashamed of the transparency of his thoughts. Much self-control is needed to finally buy the mental lucidity that awakens man and excites him up until the cheap illusion sustained by distraction and ignorance becomes dull to him. Once mental lucidity is achieved by practicing self-control, the latter is no longer a self-imposed constraint but a self-sustained satisfaction.

THE SEVEN SPIRITS OF GOD

All the virtues that have been mentioned are necessary in order to get closer to understanding because the truth is flawless, and reality has no distortions. Only then will man have found his way and have barely begun his journey; and when in the middle of the road he finally finds pleasure in his every step, he will come to know his own spirit. But if he were lacking one single virtue, the path would be unbearable and the destiny impossible to reach.

If the most compassionate man were lacking self-control, even he would remain submerged in ignorance; and if he were to develop an unbreakable degree of self-control but does not understand the value of humility, he would still be drowning in confusion. Can a bird fly with a single wing or a table stand with two legs? Likewise, the spirit of man cannot spring forth when his character lacks any of the invaluable qualities that lead to reality.

In daily life, men often say that too much of anything is bad, but within the soul, these virtues have no limits; on the contrary, man's awareness dissipates when he stagnates in one of them. The road always seems difficult for those who are lost, but it is pleasant for he who knows the way.

When the goal is to know reality in its fullness, it is not profitable to settle for a half-hearted vision. Man should always aim for the total eradication of his ignorance. The virtues of the spirit are all indispensable, and if man ignores any of them, his entire perception of reality is still flawed.

The perfect harmony of a design

From the very beginning, man was given a design whose outline he must follow to build his most exceptional work. It is a sublime master plan handed down to each person as humble instructions. Sadly, most men despise humbleness, let alone being instructed; hence, it was disparaged by many who dismissed it right away and did not even bother to take a quick look because according to their careless minds, working on such a design is not worth the effort. Others tried to build it, but the result was nothing more than a piece of decorative work, an empty box that excluded all the components that they did not comprehend, while only making use of those that were visible and beautiful before the eyes of men. But the persevering and lucid apprentice patiently analyzes the design until he understands the function of each particular element, and at the end of his work, with great amazement, he observes how all the pieces collaborate with each other in a fine and coordinated way with the purpose of performing a task that only an extraordinary machine is able to do. The function is one, but the components required to carry it out are many; the spirit is one, but many are the virtues that sustain it.

One day a great sailing ship left for the new world. Being already at high seas, the captain discovered that three members of the crew were conspiring to change the course of the vessel. As a result, the captain proceeded according to the maritime law that gave him authority to sentence to death anyone who was part of a riot. The rest of the crew agreed with the sentence handed down by the captain, except for the boatswain that was in charge of keeping the boat in optimum condition.

After seeing this, the captain said to the entire crew: "Can you believe that a boatswain is opposing the sentence imposed by me? He doubts my good judgment and has forgotten that everyone here trusts me because I'm just and righteous. I would never put your lives at risk! I'm neither a drunk nor a glutton. I'm a faithful follower of God and a steadfast man. Much prestige I have acquired because of my great accomplishments. Not for nothing was I chosen as captain of this great ship."

The boatswain then replied: "It is evident that you have many attributes, but a machine is still useless when it lacks a single one of its essential parts. I am aware of your good fame and reputation before the eyes of men, but what you call righteousness and determination is actually a lack of mercy; you are well-versed in positions of authority, but you are unaware of the power of simplicity. Can anyone repair his faults if his hands are busy applauding his own virtues? A wise man is more concerned about the weaknesses he still has to overcome than the strengths he has already developed.

"That which is already routine work in this sailing ship is precisely what you need to grasp. Those who built this ship did not hand it over until they had hammered the very last nail because they knew that each piece was vital to ensure the integrity of the machine. If the rope of the ship's wheel is loose, it becomes impossible to maneuver the vessel; if we did not have ballast weight in the hold of the vessel, the buoyant force would overturn the ship; if the tall masts and sails were not well secured, we would not be able to harness the wind; and if any gap within the ship's hull were not properly covered during caulking, water could easily sink the boat. Each and every one of these structures is needed in order to have the direction, the stability, the thrust and the resistance to reach the destination. Oh, captain! You would never dare to sail if the ship was missing a single one of those four components. If you are so cautious with a machine made of wood, why not with your own soul? Be compassionate. By showing mercy, a man is benevolent not just to his neighbor's soul; he is also being kind to his own soul that is always begging for sanity."

Before the boatswain could finish, the captain interrupted him, saying that the death sentence would be carried out to set a categorical example for the others. They proceeded with the order and executed the three conspirators. Then, the captain said to the crew: "Do not be afraid. This ship will always be safe while it's under my command. Has anyone ever seen a boatswain that is wiser than a captain?"

WHEN THE THUNDERS SPEAK

With an afflicted voice, the boatswain replied: "And who has ever seen such a thing? That even after having traveled around the entire world, man remains stagnant; even with his impressive ships, he continues adrift. You consider yourself a righteous man, but you are crippled. Cruelty and indifference are only symptoms. The disease is ignorance. Thus, what good are the other virtues if by themselves they are not able to cure the disease?"

It does not make any difference whether one person snatches a life secretly or one does it in public supported by his laws; both are murderers. He who does not practice mercy is not able to know what it means to be alive, for he is unaware of the immense value that all life brings with it and its ability to restore itself. When the essential nature of mercy is ignored, all other virtues of man are similar to a luxurious ship that, despite its apparent sturdiness and beauty, ends up at the bottom of the sea because a small flaw was overlooked during its construction. Humankind was given the design of an unparalleled machine whose integrity does not come from wood or metal, but no device is able to come alive until its construction is finished. Life is given, but the spirit must be built.

3

THE HERD, THE SOCIETY

Revelation is a unique book in its class, not because of its complex and mysterious words but due the powerful message behind them. To understand its meaning, it is necessary to abandon our herd mentality; it is imperative to restore the discernment that we have voluntarily rendered to the convenience of having others decide for us. At some point, we will have to understand that self-discernment is one of the most valuable gifts given to human beings, and each individual must put it into practice without worrying too much about being rejected by others. An exercised discernment always leads to the truth, but relying on the discernment of others weakens the conscience. If you want to understand the truth, instead of following the herd blindly, exercise your discernment so that you are able to trust your conscience.

Running without direction

Men have sold their discernment; they have surrendered it to those who use vain explanations to justify their carnal and emotional weaknesses. There are serpents that we call guides, but they are teachers without a lesson to give, knives without a sharp edge. We tend to use each other to justify our weaknesses so that any guilt is mutually suppressed, thus ensuring the permanence of our habits.

Society is a herd in which each animal prefers to follow the majority to avoid being left alone and vulnerable. Survival instincts and fear force animals to travel in groups to improve the likelihood of preserving their life in the midst of predators or the inclemency of nature, but too frequently, for humans in particular, pure convenience is what drives their behavior. We act as a group of unconscious creatures in which each individual limits himself to doing only what the collective mind of society commands him to do. The problem is that the collective mind is nothing more than the sum of minds that think alike and not necessarily the sum of minds that think correctly.

The relative morality of society is similar to a man that walks with a limp; it steps firmly with one foot but lightly and feeble with the other. Society's morality condemns robbery, but it praises those who abuse the labor of the poor. It condemns eating dog meat but is indifferent to the suffering of other animals. It condemns the prostitute, but it tries to justify its own addiction to pornography. It condemns violence but maltreats those in prison. It condemns liars but loves morbid circumstances and gossip. It loudly advocates for love but hates its enemies. Society is a lame man, and relativism is the cane that sustains its weaknesses.

While pretending to be irreproachable, society uses the most audacious and persuasive arguments to justify the habits of the majority, but, in the end, even the most exquisite eloquence contradicts itself when it lacks sincerity; only in the inquisitive and disinterested heart is contradiction never to be found.

Those who destroy lives with violence and steal in the dark already have someone that admonishes them; society itself is trying to bring them to sanity. But who will bring society to sanity? For it disguises its homicides with deceit and steals with persuasion in plain sight, and we are all accomplices. Even if the majority consents to legalize injustice, it continues to be injustice as long as there are victims.

The morality of society requires the most audacious lawyers because many of its norms are full of contradictions that change from time to time and from culture to culture, supported only by fancy words that are able to decorate the emptiest arguments. For many, the most outrageous lies become an appeasing truth when it is convenient for their own comfort, which they believe is sufficient to justify their relativism; while spiritual truth is objective and never needs justification because it is justice in itself. Some say that everything in life is relative, but, even though this is particularly the case for traditions and customs, the more we reflect with an equitable mind concerning our own ways, the more we realize that the truth is one. Otherwise, it would not be the truth. Indeed, absolute truth exists, but it does not have a name nor a master; instead of trying to determine who has it, man must find out what it is. Those who live according to such truth do so in an unbiased and disinterested manner precisely because the only way to find it is through sincere gratitude for existence and never through customs or traditions.

The content of the Book of Revelation warns about deceptions, conflicts and confusion, about false prophets that persuade and control crowds and strange creatures with power and dominion to torment men. Immense power is attributed to these figures, and although their authority was granted to them in a very distant past, their dominion persists up to this day both over religious people as much as over atheists, over Muslims as much as over Christians and Jews. The influence of those characters described in Revelation has subjugated the spirit of man over generations, but their power cannot stand by itself; it simply feeds on the herd mentality that men insist on assuming.

WHEN THE THUNDERS SPEAK

In order to truly understand the message of Revelation, it is necessary to get out of the comfort zone and stay away from the notion that we belong to a herd that we have become accustomed to follow unconsciously. As it is the case with animals, moving away from the group also poses a risk for any man, who may end up in an even worse situation if he is not well prepared; when he is left alone and does not have the tools to defend himself, he becomes an easy prey of his own wickedness. On the other hand, when in the midst of his reflection man realizes that the herd has lost its way, and he decides to follow his conscience instead, even if he is left alone, there will be no predator that could devour him because his discernment drives away his own voracious ego.

Dare to challenge your own conceptions and those of our society; perception and tastes change when you continually exercise true discernment. Ordinary desires arise from a spoiled mind and its distortions, which seem to be real and normal just because most men have the exact same weaknesses.

Revelation was written by a man who knew thoroughly the teachings of Jesus, whose words were incomprehensible to a large part of society from that time and, to some degree, continue to be for the society of today. Many concepts have been forgotten. We have confined the teachings of Jesus to only his sacrifice and instructions about loving the neighbor, and we have not even tried to understand those to their full extent.

When a human being prefers to walk blindly, letting himself to be guided by others according to prejudices that are the children of traditions, he makes the same error that a group of men committed around two thousand years ago, when they shouted: "Free Barabbas ... crucify Jesus!" Perhaps we are no longer able to murder someone with our own hands, but with our ignorance we still condemn to death those teachings that are capable of giving life to men. We behave like this in the name of society, which we follow blindly

THE HERD, THE SOCIETY

wherever it goes, launching cruel attacks on any individual who tries to get us out of our usual ignorance. Behaving as a herd could be beneficial for saving the physical life in situations of imminent danger or for the sake of the social convenience that we obtain from being surrounded by like-minded people, but it is highly detrimental to our primary goal of developing self-discernment. Saving our bodies is of no use if our minds prefer to be dead.

Although society appears to have become more civilized and technology and science are moving forward at an accelerating pace, man is slowing down to a halt when it comes to uncovering the mysteries within his conscience and the awareness of his own existence. Even in ordinary matters related to ethics and morals, the progress that has been achieved so far came about after thousands of years of unjust acts that society itself considered to be acceptable. And yet, after all the overwhelming mistakes that we have made, there persists the notion that selfishness and arrogance are qualities that each individual must have in order to find happiness and reach abundance; but vanity alone is what has been found, and the only thing overflowing is indifference.

The dubious decency of the collective mind

There was once a small hamlet of farmers and bakers who worked the wheat from its cultivation up to when the bread came out of the oven. Neighboring villages were always eager to buy their bread and flour, and the hamlet was thriving, but working the wheat in large quantities was an exhausting job that consumed all their energy and most of their time.

One day, the heads of the families of the hamlet assembled their people and said: "day after day our sons break their backs harvesting the wheat under the scorching sun, while our daughters and wives spend long hours preparing the bread. So much work is unbearable and unfair, and we can no longer suffer to see the field draining the life out of us in this manner. Keeping our families in such conditions is immoral. We need to get rid of this great burden. We have always been able to harness the power of wild animals for our own advantage, and we must find a way to do it again."

These men then departed on a quest to find a remedy. Several months later, they returned with a group of strangers who right away were put to work. The heads of the families were received with applause and praise, and everyone rejoiced greatly. They prospered even more and lived happily ever after, at least according to what they believed to be happiness. As for the group of strangers that they brought to work the fields with shackles tied to their feet, nobody really cared. Thus, not many people knew what their fate was, much less what happened to their children, whom they had to abandon forever.

Some of those strangers were able to keep their sanity but lost all authority over their bodies; others managed to maintain authority over their own bodies but lost their lives; in any case, they were deprived of the few things that a human being actually owns. Plunder and cruelty are everywhere before our eyes, but indifference is blind to the core.

Such a story would seem like a fable, but it was more real than the superficial life that most of us are living today. It was not just a small hamlet; it was entire nations that consented to slavery, and it was not only one generation that profited from the abuse, but during millennia, cruelty was the unquestionable norm as if reason did not exist and mercy was heresy. The worst part is that we have not learned the lesson yet; we continue to accept all other inherited customs without questioning our habits, and with a null discernment we run incessantly towards a cliff. Injustice and plunder are still the norm. The only thing that changes is the victim.

For a long time, a great number of men came to assert that it was impossible to abolish slavery on the grounds that doing so

THE HERD, THE SOCIETY

would bring about, supposedly, the total debacle of society, whose economy and habits were based on that absurdity. This is a perfect example of the dangers that arise from endorsing all the customs accepted by the majority. Our eagerness to satisfy ourselves increasingly distorts reality until we reach a point in which we become blind in every respect to the suffering of others. Indifference is the most blatant accomplice of injustice.

Society may claim credit for having succeeded in abolishing slavery, and we might boast about how righteous we have become, but the truth of the matter is that we have been condoning and promoting the miseries of slavery for over four thousand years. And its abolition was not achieved by us but in spite of us, when a few men dared to oppose our customs, enduring countless humiliations while their blood served as food for our comfort.

This is how society, the herd, acts. We are an immense stampede of animals in which each man runs illogically in the same direction as the rest for the simple reason that they are a majority, and anyone who stops and ponders taking another path is run over without delay by the large wave of animals that never changes direction.

When most men share the same vices and weaknesses, a level of uniformity is created within the habits of the group that makes their behaviors seem straight, no matter how crooked they may be.

Why wait for others to show us the right path when the collective mind of society has proven to have a great inability to exercise discernment? Not only were we responsible for bringing slavery into a world where every creature is born free, but we also subjugated women for the sole purpose of ensuring man's comfort; with great violence, we conquered nations who never threatened us; we have massacred entire communities of indigenous people while invading their lands, often to the point of completely erasing their culture; we were also the ones who killed the great teachers of antiquity who thousands of years ago tried to remove the blindfold that with pride we placed over our eyes, and centuries later, when we found out that Jesus was in custody, we were quick to yell out "crucify him!", and then we martyred his followers as well.

Such evils would not have persisted for so many years without the consent of the majority of us, who either tolerated or were part of such atrocities. If we were honest with ourselves, we would have to admit that we would have also made the same mistakes that our ancestors committed, for we continue to walk blindly according to what the majority dictates; the only difference between our ancestors and us is that our generation was fortunate enough to have been born after the crucial social changes that sharpened humanity's perception in relation to the injustices of the past. However, the muscles of our discernment are still atrophied; we have learned to reject the injustices of the past not because of our own consciousness as individuals, but because we have been raised in a less hostile environment where the injustices that come from those old customs have become obvious.

We have not learned to discern by ourselves; we continue to think that everything that is legal is acceptable. We behave like a man who, after having overcome a strong addiction to a particular narcotic, celebrates such an accomplishment every day by getting intoxicated with other drugs while affirming that he has recovered his sanity at last.

With its well-trained indifference, society proudly builds altars to opulence. The conquest of the new world was a triumph for the conquerors but a great misfortune for those conquered; the pyramids of Giza are extraordinary marvels before our eyes, but they were an enormous calamity for the slaves who spent decades building them; the invention of the atomic bomb was an exciting discovery for science, but it was an immense catastrophe for the inhabitants of Hiroshima and Nagasaki.

THE HERD, THE SOCIETY

Gradually, the collective mind of society has been reforming itself, but when we compare the achievements with the thousands of years that it took to achieve them, we may conclude that the collective mind is unreliable. Just as you would never take the risk of entrusting the care of your little daughter to a man with a history of pedophilia even if he seems reformed, in the same manner, you should never entrust the care of your discernment to a society that has committed, and still commits, so many atrocities.

When our customs are challenged, instead of turning into a mad stampede that tramples and stomps, we should resort to our own discernment to keep us from panicking so that we have a clear sight of the path.

Restoring discernment

The customs inherited from society must be questioned one by one, bearing in mind that truth and reason supersede tradition. The ignorance of man is a disease that can only be healed with an inquisitive mind and an independent judgment.

Human beings are blindfolded by desire and habit, and they will appoint as their master anyone who can guarantee the continuity of these two things; that man becomes the leader of the tribe. But a guide is not someone who finds you in a place and tells you to stay in the same spot. When you cannot find a guide capable of leading you to the next destination, do not stand still waiting for one. Just get out of wherever you are. You will probably advance if you just start walking using as your compass the sense of empathy, self-improvement and purpose.

And if you were lucky enough to find a true guide, never expect to stay under his wings. The good guide is a disinterested friend with the goal of teaching you how to find the right path on your own. If you had the misfortune of falling into the hands of the self-seeking false guide, learn to identify him before you end up wasting your life walking in circles; the self-seeking guide wants you to depend on him forever because his ego is bigger than his advice.

Many people prefer guides that seem strict in some matters but are sweet talkers in others. Men decide to become disciples of those who simply tell them what they already want to hear. They follow them because they hold dear the superficiality of the material world, the splendid flattery of people and the impressive demonstration of power. Humility and simplicity have no value for them, or even worse, such qualities are looked at with disdain, scorn and mockery. To be admired and be seen as their leader, one must merely justify the pleasures and vices of the vast majority while condemning only the most obvious transgressions in order to comfort their conscience and appease any feelings of guilt. In such a way, many end up choosing as their guides men and women who simply think alike. The false sense of peace provided by the justifier of weaknesses leads them to think that they have finally found the truth; they survive and thrive socially, but their souls slowly wither.

We place our trust in these false guides because, in doing so, it becomes easier for us to get rid of all responsibility and guilt. Man has been endowed with the invaluable ability to discern for himself but chooses to do everything as if he were part of a herd, no matter how absurd this behavior may be. Since when does a man need another man to think for him? Man asserts that he has the right to rule over the beasts of the earth, but he cannot stop acting like one of them.

If the most admired, most decorated and most authoritative person in this society were to assure you, along with the majority of men, that the only way to save your brother's soul is by stoning him to death, would you do it? Man's conscience was not created to kneel before a multitude, much less before tyrants. However, for simple convenience or out of fear of being wrong, man defines his goals and values based on what the majority considers correct without

THE HERD, THE SOCIETY

questioning such norms at all. As we grow old, we expect society to teach us what is right when, in fact, society itself is full of ignorance.

The feeling of well-being and protection obtained from society often becomes a deception in which man, like cattle, eats and sleeps but lacks the stimulus to develop his mind and, stupefied, is taken to the slaughterhouse without realizing that he never got to live. In this manner, entire generations have come and gone without understanding the most basic principles of the spirit.

In ancient times, war, bloody as it was, was regarded as honorable by many, and the leaders who decided to conquer other nations, despite the high price of human lives, were seen as brave and wise men worthy of imitation and even of worship. When the conquering leader returned to his kingdom, he was greeted with applause and compliments by his people, and very few wondered about the suffering of those who were defeated.

Society has found ways to openly promote deception by condemning the vices that destroy in an instant but enjoying those that destroy the body and mind slowly. Yet, many decide to follow the majority without hesitation because it is terrifying for them to be left alone; even so, the spirit is strong, and its essence is too ancient to be fooled by the irrational immaturity of society.

Meanwhile, it is impossible to see clearly while staying in the midst of the herd, and the only way to change its direction is by running faster than the ones at the front. The truth-seeking mind should not follow the collective mind all the time. It must learn to make decisions on its own and exercise its discernment. It is immoral to have another person decide for you what is morally acceptable.

Our minds are numbed due to all the entertainment and anxiety that surround us in this modern era. The average man works for a third of the day; during another third, his main concern is deciding which distraction to choose to appease his mind; he then falls asleep for the remaining third, and he repeats the same routine the next day. The only thing different is the type of entertainment that he chooses from the immense variety that is available to him, but the vain and illusory nature of the routine does not change.

All these distractions harden the hearts of the great majority of the people, for whom deceit becomes their reality over time. The difference between righteousness and immorality has no meaning when reality is blurred by a widespread deception that is continually reinforced by our sense of belonging to the majority. What is an irrefutable lie in the intimacy of the conscience often disguises itself as truth in the collective mind.

Despite this lack of reasoning, there have always been men and women that understood the true meaning of mercy, righteousness, self-control and unbiased love, and they dared to condemn the falsehoods of the majority even if that meant being left alone against kings, priests and judges. Often, they were considered apostates and perverters of the law and sentenced to death by the same wandering people they were trying to enlighten. Many were lapidated by those that most needed them. Risking their own lives for the simple reason of stating the truth might appear like a foolish act, but the fact that we are still learning from them even to this day proves that their efforts served a great purpose for which we should be grateful.

But we also learn from the people around us, from our parents, brothers and friends; then we learn from more distant leaders, whether from the community, politics or religion. When they no longer have anything to teach us, we then inquire into writings from the past; but the search for the truth should not end there because its magnitude cannot be contained within the totality of books that have been written or within the number of teachers who have spoken. The essential truth is too great to be understood through words and too simple to be understood by the ego. After depleting all the external sources, there comes a point in time when a man's reflection must become his own teacher and his judgment his training field.

Any attitude that promotes a numb conscience must be discarded. Allowing unjust acts to be established as norms is not discipline; it is indifference.

Making use of your own discernment will not guarantee you an easy and harmonious life with others; on the contrary, very often, it will put you into uncomfortable situations in which you will be seen as a stranger among close friends. Whenever the herd finds out that there is something within it that threatens to change its habits, it quickly becomes a stampede that runs over anything that is not moving in the same direction.

Self-discernment has always been the only way to identify the changes that society needs, even more so when making your stance known could end up being the cause of your death. When the intolerance of men is irritated by the truth, it often turns into violence. It happened with Martin Luther King Jr. when he was murdered for opposing racial segregation; with John F. Kennedy when he intended to fight against hypocrisy and secrecy; with Gandhi for trying to have people from two different religions coexist in peace; and it is illustrated in the story of Jesus when he is crucified for not surrendering his resolution to show us the ultimate truth.

Now we boast of righteousness by saying that we would have never lifted a finger against those men we have mentioned, when the reality is that they died because of their efforts to dismantle systems that were, or continue to be, our most precious treasures; that is, they gave their lives to oppose traditions and habits that we protect with passion. We might not have pulled the trigger, but we would most certainly have pointed our fingers at those people to identify them as a threat to our society.

WHEN THE THUNDERS SPEAK

The message of Revelation is on the horizon, and you just have to keep advancing to see it, but when you keep your head down, blindly following the footsteps of others, you cannot even notice from where the sun rises. The truth is clear and simple. Otherwise, it would not be true; it is bad habits and traditions that obscures it. To understand it to its fullest extent, you must make way and run faster than the herd; only then will you be in a position to see everything that is ahead of you and decide for yourself where you want to go.

The principles of the soul are not to be embraced blindly; all its attributes can be confirmed by logic as long as the mind of man is clear of vices and prejudice. If there is order in the physical universe, there is much more order in the spiritual realm. The mind is designed to seek order in all things, but if self-discernment is never put into practice, it will undoubtedly believe that order can only be found by satisfying its weaknesses. Only when man ceases to treat his vices and obsessions as if they were needs will he be able to clear his mind to understand what order is made of and what are the dominions of chaos, ignorance and death.

4

SEALED BOOK

The great expectation

> *I saw, in the right hand of him who sat on the throne, a book written inside and outside, sealed shut with seven seals. I saw a mighty angel proclaiming with a loud voice, "Who is worthy to open the book, and to break its seals?" No one in heaven above, or on the earth, or under the earth, was able to open the book, or to look in it. (Revelation 5:1-3)*

Since ancient times, the search for truth has been a path that many have tried to take in all corners of the earth. The sublime meaning of existence has always caused perplexity to men who have dared to conceive it, but the vast majority of people end up surrendering their search for understanding to superficial traditions and concepts that numerous cultures have used throughout history to explain what they do not understand.

However, something different was happening in Judea and Galilee in the first century. Although many people were expecting a Jewish liberator who by means of armed conflict or politics would restore the glory of Israel in worldly terms, many others were expecting a Messiah or event that would bring along the understanding that they had been waiting for quite a long time. Someone who could nourish their minds and free their souls. These men preserved the teachings of the emissaries of antiquity and had serious doubts about various vain and unjust customs and norms that the rest of the people adopted with the strictest discipline and an unbreakable devotion.

Such a situation forced them to hide their way of thinking from the rest since it was contrary to laws that were considered sacred by most men, who would never hesitate to use the cruelest methods to purge the supposed evil out of those who did not obey their traditions.

Asking obvious and simple questions could be enough to get an entire town to stone you to death. Those who had such concerns had to remain in a community that grew under the shadows of society, while out in the open, the entire political-religious system was dominated, and it still is to some degree, by the power of the false prophet. The beast could decide who would die and who would live, or even worse, had the power to decide what was right and what was wrong. And today, although the false prophet has limited authority to kill the physical body, he still maintains its power to decide what is good and virtuous, and with deception, he has led hundreds of millions of people to spiritual death.

Great perplexity tormented the few men who really took pains to find the truth. It was incomprehensible to them that since the time of the ancient prophets, generation after generation, the most righteous men were precisely those who ended up being victims of the violent laws of the rulers and priests, who, with the support of the people and following the instructions of their writings, condemned to death or exile every soul that uttered wise words against their norms or traditions.

For the righteous men, it was incomprehensible that for more than 500 years, the truth had been trampled and humiliated by vile lies; it was inconceivable to them that the majority of the people still did not understand the words of mercy and integrity of the emissaries of antiquity; it was difficult for them to believe that laws so mundane and unjust were attributed to the Giver of Life; and it was also difficult for them to imagine having to live in the shadows for the rest of their lives just because the behavior that they knew was right, for the rest of the people, turned out to be the most sinister heresy.

Uncertainty and violence were the only things that awaited those men who, in their search for the truth, opposed the rules of the people. In such a situation, there was a never-ending expectation concerning the arrival of someone that would finally vindicate them and take them out of the shadows. They hoped for a teacher that would reveal the knowledge needed to reach the ultimate truth, and that would be able to turn the indifference of many into true devotion for compassion, but, for the moment, the rest of the men continued to be servants of deceitfulness and worshipers of vanity.

With the truth cut off, the book of life was sealed, and with it had been sealed the understanding of the past and the wisdom to comprehend the eternal truth of the present. On the other hand, the book that certainly remained open before the eyes of everyone was that of vain traditions and ancient writings of the people, which with grotesque rites and cruel laws rather resembled a book of sorcery and black magic. Writings so cruel that even dared to say that it was an honorable behavior to instruct a crowd to take stones in their hands, surround a helpless soul and then stone her until the body, unable to withstand the severe wounds, ends up giving its last breath of life in the midst of such violence. Writings so idolatrous that ordered people to cut the throat of thousands of animals with the alleged purpose of pleasing or obtaining the forgiveness of the Creator, or, supposedly, to symbolize a gesture of sacrifice, when, in fact, the only thing that is being sacrificed is mercy and sanity while they build an altar to idolatry and indifference. What good is it if in order to maintain a ritual's symbolism, the practitioner must renounce other virtues that are much more important than the ritual itself?

How to reconcile the fact that the emissaries of the truth called for mercy and meekness, but the god of the people demanded blood and power? How was it possible that for more than 500 years, the path of righteousness and truth was being consumed by the flames of lies and ignorance?

All those unknowns kept awake at night a group of men and women who were waiting for someone who would answer all their questions; someone that would lead them to uncover the mysteries of the past and show them the way to reign over the present; someone who would reveal to them the definitive teachings that would clarify all doubts about existence.

That character would not take much longer to come, but during the time just before his arrival, that small community found refuge in the words of John the Baptist, who, while preaching in desert regions outside of Jerusalem, made it his personal responsibility to train their ears so that they could understand those teachings they would have the privilege to receive later on. John the Baptist assured them that someone would eventually open the incomprehensible book of life and reveal its content for the benefit of the true Jews and all of mankind.

Coming out of the shadows

Fear and uncertainty started to dissipate when the seekers of the truth heard about someone from the Judean desert who was shouting the words that for generations they had been waiting for. With his message of redemption and forgiveness of sins, John the Baptist became the hope for those who knew the truth, and those regions where he preached became the place where men with similar thoughts could congregate and speak freely.

But, at the same time, John the Baptist represented a great affront to the rulers and priests of Jerusalem, who claimed that the forgiveness of sins was only possible through the bloody rites that were performed exclusively in the temple. This obviously contrasted with the actions of John and his message, which stated that a man is already forgiven if he has a repentant heart and a sincere determination to straighten his ways. His baptism did not require money or the blood of animals.

Without anything to offer in return, men and women from all over Judea came to the Jordan River with a sincere desire to reform their lives. They were met by someone who affirmed that each one of them had the opportunity to start from scratch. This was within their reach without having to set foot in the Temple of Jerusalem. Undoubtedly, John the Baptist was a threat to the dominant religious system, and although the writings claim that his execution was due to his strong criticism of the questionable relationship between Herod and Herodias, there are enough reasons to believe that both Pharisees and Sadducees had a marked interest in getting rid of the prophet.

After John's arrest and subsequent beheading by Herod, the Pharisees and Sadducees probably thought that the prophet's followers would disperse and that his words would be forgotten.

However, the death of John the Baptist did not stop the thirst for knowledge; what was happening in the minds of men and women was greater than the life of the prophet and more extensive than the desert of Judea. They were still waiting for the one that would take them out of the shadows and would vindicate the emissaries of the truth, whom they called true prophets of antiquity and who were ignored and often murdered by their own people. They kept waiting for those wise teachings because they knew that the words preached by the Pharisees and Sadducees did not come from the light. The great expectation continued, and the uncertainty was growing.

Worthy to open the scroll

The "god" that was created by man prefers ignorant soldiers because he wants to empower himself, while the God that has always existed set in motion an entire creation and an immutable truth just to empower his children.

> *And I wept much because no one had been found worthy to open the book nor to regard it. And one of the elders says to me, Do not weep. Behold, the lion which is of the tribe of Juda, the root of David, has overcome so as to open the book, and its seven seals. (Revelation 5:4-5)*

With these words, the author of the Book of Revelation introduces the Prince of Peace, whose teachings would put an end to the expectation of those that had been waiting for the arrival of a man who had the understanding to discern the mysteries of existence. A figure that would answer the great enigmas and contradictions that afflict the spirit of man; someone who would bring clarity to the confusion that existed around the inconsistencies found in the traditions and ancient writings of the land of Canaan.

While the deception of the past was still reigning, the laws and certain writings of antiquity not only rewarded the arrogance that proudly feeds the indifference of men, but they also pretended to purify their dirty souls with vain rites that had only served to sink them more into the false notion that their paths of violence were right. Writings and traditions that demand great violence and try to incarnate the divinity in the most mundane vanities by using great temples, sumptuous garments, impetuous behavior and superficial solemn events.

SEALED BOOK

But vanity can never beautify the spirit. It can only suffocate it with its burdens. And an act of cruelty can never be justified by blind faith because it is always better to be pious and have faith in mercy than to be cruel while having faith in what is not understood.

However, the faithful followers of the beast, even after millennia, blindly continue to justify those bloody acts and cruel laws, arguing that they represent things that go beyond our comprehension and that the people and their leaders did well by stoning to death those who violated their foolish norms. They even dare to say that those men were killed because it was commanded by divine laws. The faithful followers of the beast ignore that mercy, forgiveness and the opportunity to rehabilitate are the true divine decrees, and these principles are certainly within the reach of man's understanding. Only those who live in darkness would dare to tear those principles apart by sacrificing them in honor of that which they admit they do not understand.

The arrival of Jesus was necessary because the deception of the beast was immense, and it is all over us up to this day, considering that we still follow its most mundane instructions and its most dishonest examples to justify our own weaknesses. Today, even its most cruel and dark ordinances are still carried out by many, such as taking the life of another man, and the rest who do not, in any case, pretend to justify those actions alleging that circumstances of that time so warranted.

When we try to affirm that cruel laws and sterile traditions were instituted by God, and we pretend to ascribe an exceedingly mundane behavior to the Creator, we deny ourselves the opportunity to know Him in all His splendor because we shelter in our hearts the imperfections and the indifference that are required to justify atrocious acts committed against our own brothers. In turn, such an attitude alienates us from true wisdom and makes us stagnate spiritually with a heart of stone that will never have the ability to see or feel the true wonders of creation.

Men were in a state of confusion that did not allow them see the path that leads to truth and understanding. Day and night, their souls were afflicted by the religious leaders who, with writings supposedly dictated by God, forced them to be unmerciful and indifferent. Darkness was dense, and the lovers of ignorance were many, but the truth would soon find a way to manifest itself before men.

> *I saw in the midst of the throne and of the four living creatures, and in the midst of the elders, a Lamb standing, as though it had been slain, having seven horns, and seven eyes, which are the seven Spirits of God, sent out into all the earth. Then he came, and he took it out of the right hand of him who sat on the throne. Now when he had taken the book, the four living creatures and the twenty-four elders fell down before the Lamb...They sang a new song, saying, "You are worthy to take the book, and to open its seals: For you were killed, and bought us for God with your blood, out of every tribe, language, people, and nation. (Revelation 5:6-9)*

Certainly, a man would come that would change everything. Jesus took the book and showed it to the world; he revealed the meaning of existence and fought against those who profited from ignorance; he uttered words forbidden by the powerful and declared those ones expected by the meek; he unmasked the false prophets of antiquity and stripped off the deceitfulness from history.

5

HORSEMEN OF CANAAN

As we move towards the main story written in the Book of Revelation, a series of imagery and symbolism starts to emerge that lead to the message conveyed in the letter. At first, it may seem futile trying to make sense of all the symbolism when there are so many different concepts it could represent, but the reader must be patient and understand that only after coming across the central hidden message—which is presented herein in later chapters—will he be able to see with clarity how all the other elements and details fall into place to support the whole narrative.

The main story starts when the Lamb proceeds to unroll the scroll and begins to open its seven seals. As this happens, the author of Revelation sees four horsemen come forth, one for each of the first four seals.

The four horsemen that emerge with the opening of the first four seals represent events that characterized the history of the region of Canaan until the destruction of the first Temple of Jerusalem and the exile of its ruling and priestly class to Babylon. Such events shaped the culture and religion of the kingdoms of Israel and Judah.

The key to understanding the meaning of the four horsemen lies in the fact that each horseman is introduced by one of the four living creatures that were standing around the throne. By following the same order in which the four living creatures were described in chapter 4 of Revelation, the first creature, which is similar to a lion, introduces the first horseman; while the creature that is like a calf announces the second horseman; then the creature that has the face of a man introduces the third, and, finally, the creature that is like a flying eagle introduces the fourth horseman.

Faithful and True

> And I saw when the Lamb opened one of the seven seals, and I heard one of the four living creatures saying as with a voice of thunder, Come. And I saw, and behold, a white horse, and he that sat thereon had a bow; and there was given unto him a crown: and he came forth conquering, and to conquer. (Revelation 6:1-2)

The first horseman, who rides a white horse, is introduced by the first living creature, which is similar to a lion, not only because it was the first of the four living creatures to be described previously but also because John had already used the image of the lion to associate Jesus with the tribe of Judah; furthermore, the author describes the voice of this particular living creature as a voice of "thunder," which is a term that he uses on multiple occasions when referring to the authority of the Creator.

Later on, in the final chapters of the book, the author of Revelation himself explains the meaning of the horseman on a white horse:

> I saw the heaven opened, and behold, a white horse, and he who sat on it is called Faithful and True. In righteousness he judges and makes war. His eyes are a flame of fire, and on his head are many crowns. He has names written and a name written which no one

knows but he himself. He is clothed in a garment sprinkled with blood. His name is called "The Word of God." (Revelation 19:11-13)

Since the time when ignorance became the judge of the people, the few men and women who have dared to defend the truth have been victims of ridicule, torture and even assassination by those who claim to know the Creator. The powerful do not get tired of trampling the meek, the cruel find it necessary to torture the merciful, and the hypocrites mock those who have self-control. However, the Word of God will still be visible on the horizon when the storm dies down.

When referring to the Word of God, the Gospel of John says: "In the beginning was the Word, and the Word was with God, and the Word was God. The same was in the beginning with God." For that reason, the vision of the white horse corresponds to the first seal. Considering that the Word of God is known as the beginning and the end, the author of Revelation uses the same concept to indicate a point of reference in history: the beginning of all things.

With the triumphant reappearance of the white horse in the final chapters, the entire vision of Revelation is enclosed within what is defined as the beginning and the end: the Word of God. Indicating that at the end of the story, despite all the injustices and calamities, the truth will prevail, and the purpose of creation would be fulfilled.

The Word of God is the truth that was present long before written texts and that has always been an essential part of man in his journey towards understanding; perfecting his conscience every day according to what he is capable of discerning. It is the true intention of creation, a voice that emanates from the sincere reflection of anyone. The Word of God can be seen in the exceptional deeds of men; sometimes it is embodied in books, and other times is transmitted by word of mouth, but it will never belong to a particular religion alone. That is the Word of God, beyond human patent, with no religion, present from the beginning and triumphant at the end.

Conflict between two kingdoms

> *And when he opened the second seal, I heard the second living creature saying, Come. And another horse came forth, a red horse: and to him that sat thereon it was given to take peace from the earth, and that they should slay one another: and there was given unto him a great sword. (Revelation 6:3-4)*

The horseman on the red horse represents the periods of war that occurred in the region of Canaan between the kingdoms of Judah and Israel. This horseman is introduced by the second living creature, which is similar to a calf, a symbol that has always been used to illustrate the rupture of the first Kingdom of Israel and the constant wars that took place between the two kingdoms that emerged from its division: Judah in the south and Israel in the north.

The first book of Kings, chapter 12, explains how Jeroboam, who had just been proclaimed King of Israel by the northern tribes, builds two golden calves and places them in the cities of Bethel and Dan in order to establish the two new religious centers of worship that were meant to replace the Temple of Jerusalem, which was under the authority of his adversary the King of Judah. The creation of the golden calves and the establishment of a new priestly order in the cities of Bethel and Dan marked the definitive moment in which the northern tribes became independent from the tribe of Judah, and Jerusalem ceased to be the center of worship for those who decided to form the new Kingdom of Israel. The following years were characterized by many armed conflicts and conspiracies between those two peoples who were brothers.

HORSEMEN OF CANAAN

The temple's scale

> *And when it opened the third seal, I heard the third living creature saying, Come and see. And I saw: and behold, a black horse, and he that sat upon it having a balance in his hand. And I heard as a voice in the midst of the four living creatures saying, "A choenix of wheat for a denarius, and three choenixes of barley for a denarius: and do not injure the oil and the wine." (Revelation 6:5-6)*

Many have tried to associate that phrase with times of scarcity and hunger; however, a denarius was not an exorbitant amount of money. Its value was close to one day's salary; while the Greek measure χοῖνιξ (choenix) was more than two pounds of wheat, which was a considerable amount of food for a day. Such a situation, even though it would still be unfavorable, would not be uncommon. Furthermore, the scarcity interpretation does not explain the last part of the phrase that speaks about not injuring the oil and the wine.

Rather, the balance in the hand of the horseman on the black horse is the balance that was used to measure the offerings in the Temple of Jerusalem, while the phrase "a choenix of wheat for a denarius, and three choenix of barley for a denarius: do not injure the oil and the wine," refers to a very specific grain offering which we will discuss later.

Whereas the horseman on the white horse is the Word of God, the horseman on the black horse is its antagonist, the mundane doctrines that demand material things and sacrifices to allegedly buy the favor of God; teachings that are nothing but doctrines of men. For that reason, the third horseman is introduced by the third living creature, which has the face of a man.

The priests of antiquity claimed that the favor of God had to be bought with animal sacrifices or grain offerings. The transactions for such rituals required the regular use of a balance in order to measure the exact quantity that was stipulated in the Pentateuch.

Thus, the balance was a central instrument for the temple's doctrine since almost everything boiled down to the sacrifices or offerings that practitioners had to make, and such a measuring tool made it possible for people to buy within the temple premises what they would later take to the altar. With these transactions, Jerusalem and the temple had a guaranteed source of wealth.

According to the ancient writings of the temple, there was a law requiring a sacrifice or offering for each particular circumstance, either to have the protection of God, to receive forgiveness for some transgression committed, to give thanks, to fulfill a tradition or simply as a way of worship. In other words, salvation was purchased with material goods and idolatry.

But the vision of the black horse goes deeper into the matter when a voice coming from someone that is in the midst of the four creatures says: "A choenix of wheat for a denarius, and three choenix of barley for a denarius: and do not injure the oil and the wine."

This particular voice was making reference to a very specific kind of offering that consisted of flour alone, either of wheat or barley, and that did not require oil or the spilling of wine on the altar; contrary to the voluntary sacrifices of animals, which were accompanied by an offering of flour mixed with oil and a wine libation (Numbers 15:3-11); and also different from the sin sacrifice that was forced upon the people, and that also required the shedding of blood, except in the special case the voice is alluding to. That exception is stipulated in Leviticus 5:11-12, and it allows the poor to present a simple offering that consisted only of flour, without oil, and since it was a sin offering, it did not require the wine libation that normally accompanied the voluntary holocausts: "But if he can't afford two turtledoves or two young pigeons, then he shall bring as his offering for that in which he has sinned, one tenth of an ephah of fine flour for a sin offering. He shall put no oil on it..."

The offering of flour could be wheat or barley, and it exonerated the practitioner from the shedding of animal blood and required neither oil nor wine. That is to say, in the midst of a complex, superficial and often compulsory sacrificial system, the voice is hinting at how to avoid being part of such idolatry. Although people were often forced into performing those bloody rites, they could always resort to that particular exception which allowed them to bring a flour offering of barley or wheat without oil or wine libations, instead of the animal sacrifice of the sin offering or the voluntary sacrifices. This goes hand in hand with Jesus' attitude from previous chapters in which he rebukes two of the churches in Asia for "eating things sacrificed to idols."

That aversion to the idolatrous sacrificial system can also be found in other renowned writings such as the books of Isaiah, Hosea, Jeremiah and Micah, who openly criticized such customs. To understand their strong aversion to those traditions, we just have to imagine a modern-day church beheading thousands of animals in its altar, one by one, abhorrently staining the floor with blood while its leaders assure that with every drop we spill, we come closer to God. Idolatry is just the right word to describe such customs, which in reality are nothing more than doctrines of men.

The first destruction

> And when it opened the fourth seal, I heard the voice of the fourth living creature saying, Come and see. And I saw: and behold, a pale horse, and he that sat upon it, his name was Death, and hades followed with him; and authority was given to him over the fourth of the earth to slay with sword, and with hunger, and with death, and by the beasts of the earth. (Revelation 6:7-8)

WHEN THE THUNDERS SPEAK

Following the same sequence as the seals that preceded it, the vision of the fourth horseman is announced by the fourth living creature, which has the appearance of an eagle flying. In this case, the writer of Revelation uses the exact same expression that the Book of Ezekiel employs when describing the four calamities that plagued Jerusalem during the time it was under the threat of the Babylonian army:

> *For thus saith the Lord Jehovah: How much more when I send my four sore judgments upon Jerusalem, the sword, and the famine, and the evil beast, and the pestilence, to cut off from it man and beast! But behold, there shall be left in it those that escape, who shall be brought out of it, sons and daughters.* (Ezekiel 14:21-22)

John uses the same words as Ezekiel's book because he is referring to the same historical event: the captivity of Judah and the calamities that preceded that fact. That is why the living creature that introduces the fourth horseman has the appearance of a flying eagle since on many occasions, the Bible itself uses the eagle or a bird as a metaphor of captivity, migration or the displacement of nations; as it can be found, for example, at the end of the first chapter of the Book of Micah: "Make thee bald, and poll thee for the children of thy delights; enlarge thy baldness as the eagle, for they are gone into captivity from thee."

The captivity of Judah and the destruction of the first temple marked the end of the first half of the history of its people. The horseman on the pale horse, which is the last of the four, symbolizes that event, while the other three that preceded it are the line of events that occurred before and that were also relevant for shaping the identity of the region of Canaan.

In this manner, by using the symbolism of the four living creatures and the horsemen, the author of Revelation gradually orients the reader to the historical context of the message that he had to make known to those who were looking for answers but could not do so openly.

6

TRUE PROPHETS

Blood of prophets

For thousands of years, the word *prophet* has been misused and misunderstood by the wide majority. Most people believe that a prophet is a diviner who performs impressive signs and, with terrifying power, put his enemies under his feet; however, a true prophet is simply an advocate for justice and peace whose most precious power is having a sound mind and a kind spirit, an admonisher and not a punisher. A true prophet is just someone who is inspired enough to find the truth and too compassionate to keep it for himself; someone whose only weapon is his words and his own flesh is his shield; someone willing to teach what only a few can comprehend and willing to say what no one wants to hear; someone who is so sane that he is willing to be seen as a deranged person today for the sole purpose of bringing others to sanity tomorrow; someone who is so alive that he is not afraid of being killed but fears not being able to enlighten his own executioners.

"And when it opened the fifth seal, I saw underneath the altar the souls of them that had been slain for the word of God, and for the testimony which they held" (Revelation 6:9).

WHEN THE THUNDERS SPEAK

The souls under the altar were those who had been killed by the priests' doctrines since the time they were established until the destruction of their first temple, whose central image had always been the altar. The temple's doctrine instructed the people to shed innocent blood every time it was demanded by the intolerance of the priests, who relied on their ancient writings to justify the killing of anyone that was not in accordance with their laws and traditions.

Jesus himself stated that many of the prophets of antiquity were executed by their own people when he said: "Jerusalem, Jerusalem, the city that kills the prophets and stones those that are sent unto her" (Luke 13:34). It is not difficult to arrive at those conclusions when we take into account that the laws of the temple explicitly ordered to stone anyone who blasphemes their doctrine. The books of the Bible are the best witnesses that the true prophets openly opposed the actions of the priests and rulers of Israel and Judah, as well as their traditions, which, according to the clergy, came from a divine source.

The Bible is a great collection of books, many of which are sublime and very useful, but far from what many have argued, it is not a set of writings that are in accord with each other in its entirety; on the contrary, in many instances, the books present vast differences among themselves in terms of fundamental values. Thus, it is easy to notice strong tensions arising between different lines of thought within the same collection of books. Even though they are seen as one and the same by the churches of today, in reality, they have always been on opposite sides. While the powerful promoted superficial rites with a sense of pride and based their doctrine on cruel and authoritarian laws that tried to justify violent stories, another group of men and women followed the true prophets who cried out for the people to assume a disposition of mercy, humility and soundness of mind, and publicly abhorred the vain traditions of the priests.

TRUE PROPHETS

It is impossible to walk two paths that go in opposite directions; whoever intends to do so will end up walking back and forth without reaching any destination.

The words of the true prophets are clear and express a categorical disapproval of the ancient writings of the priests. Since the beginning of the Kingdom of Israel, there were people who opposed the official doctrine of the Temple of Jerusalem. For more than 500 years, there was an ongoing war of arguments—embedded within the words of the true prophets—about the nature of the Creator and the correct way of living in order to reach the truth.

However, opposing the laws and traditions that had been established by the powerful, even if it was done by words alone, involved a high price to bear because anyone who dared to show resentment towards the official doctrine of the people could be charged with blasphemy and end up paying with his own life. "And he that blasphemeth the name of Jehovah shall certainly be put to death; all the assembly shall certainly stone him; as well the stranger as he that is home-born, when he blasphemeth the Name, shall be put to death" (Leviticus 24:16). Because of these cruel laws, Isaiah always opposed the rulers of the kingdom and warned them by saying: "Woe unto them that decree iniquitous decrees, and to the writers that prescribe oppression, to turn away the poor from judgment, and to take away the right from the afflicted of my people" (Isaiah 10:1-2).

How much innocent blood has been shed in favor of a cruel and unfruitful law that was never decreed by the Creator, but was established by the intolerance of man and his proclivity to violence! How many men have been sacrificed in favor of ignorance! The only blood being shed was that of the innocents, and the land became saturated until it vomited.

Even when exposed to such risks, the true prophets did not remain silent, and their affection for humanity led them to publicly condemn the falsehoods of the temple priests' doctrine. One after the other, from Amos, more than 700 years BC, until the Babylonian exile with Ezekiel—not to be confused with the person who wrote Ezekiel 40-48, whose authorship has already been questioned by both Jewish and Christian scholars—, they risked their lives uttering strong words against those traditions and laws that were born out of the ignorance of man.

Their distrust of the writings of the leaders of Jerusalem can be found in the words of Jeremiah: "How do ye say, We are wise, and the law of Jehovah is with us? Behold, certainly the lying pen of the scribes hath made it falsehood" (Jeremiah 8:8). Likewise, the book that bears his name also criticizes the priests directly, saying: "the prophets prophesy falsehood, and the priests rule by their means; and my people love to have it so. But what will ye do in the end thereof?" (Jeremiah 5:31) A similar degree of distrust is shown by Micah when he says: "The heads thereof judge for reward, and the priests thereof teach for hire, and the prophets thereof divine for money" (Micah 3:11).

Their criticism of priests and rulers was well-founded, considering that the doctrinal differences were vast in relation to the sayings of the true prophets. The laws of the priests, thirsty for blood, pretended to teach righteousness with the vilest violence, declaring death to anyone who violated a tittle of their norms, from gathering wood on the Sabbath (Numbers 15:32-26) to even pronouncing words that supposedly offended their God (Leviticus 24:11-16). Yet, the Creator is not a man, that He should get offended, nor a woman, that He should be scandalized, and through the words of the true Ezekiel, He stripped bare the foolishness of the priests' writings, saying: "Say unto them, As I live, saith the Lord Jehovah, I have no pleasure in the death of the wicked; but that the wicked turn from his way and live" (Ezekiel 33:11).

TRUE PROPHETS

The doctrine of the priests was centered on the use of vain and idolatrous rites to achieve forgiveness and purity, which can be illustrated by the fact that one of their books was dedicated in its entirety to specifying in great detail the dozens of rites related to sacrifices. Isaiah, on the other hand, said to them: "To what purpose is the multitude of your sacrifices unto me? saith Jehovah. I am sated with burnt-offerings of rams, and the fat of fed beasts; and in the blood of bullocks, and of lambs, and of he-goats I take no pleasure. When ye come to appear before me, who hath required this from your hand—to tread my courts?" (Isaiah 1:11-12) And Hosea did not lack courage when he said on behalf of the Creator: "For I delight in loving-kindness, and not sacrifice; and the knowledge of God more than burnt-offerings."

Words like those were enough to get anyone condemned to death by the priests, who claimed that animal sacrifices were divine ordinances and that drawing away from them was an offense to God. But in spite of that, the true prophets never backed down and their words always opposed the superficiality and the tyranny of the priests' writings.

However, the truth was buried for a period of time when, in the middle of an ideological war, the tyrants and their followers massacred the meek of the earth, who—out of conviction—only used their words to defend themselves and renounced all forms of violence. Spilling blood has always been easy, but hiding the truth is the hardest of tasks. There will always be a way to find the truth because it is the only thing that actually exists. The writings of the true Jewish prophets were preserved with fervent passion by those who silently awaited their vindication.

Sharper than any two-edged sword

Intolerance and violence conspired to murder the truth. With stones and swords, they silenced those who watched over it, but with the progression of time all their weapons corroded, and the stoning ceased to be; while the truth was able to preserve its splendor and continues to thrive in the writings of Isaiah, Jeremiah, Hosea and the Ezekiel responsible for the first half of the book that bears his name.

The truth has been able to withstand the great violence that men unleashed against it for thousands of years; it maintained its sharp edge, and with each passing year, its precepts become more evident before the eyes of men. Time has been the judge and has vindicated the truth. Concerning the murderers, there is no memory left of them, but the words of the righteous will continue to reform lives, shape civilizations and unravel mysteries until the end of time.

"Who is wise, and he shall understand these things? intelligent, and he shall know them? For the ways of Jehovah are right, and the just shall walk in them; but the transgressors shall fall therein" (Hosea 14:9).

Although today we boast of being civilized, we are still so far away from understanding, that it seems as if our customs and laws had been conceived by cavemen when we were to compare them with the teachings of self-control and mercy of those men who came to know the truth more than two millennia ago. Even with all the conveniences of this modern age, we continue submerged in ignorance and lack the interest of knowing the purpose of existence. In contrast, barefooted men wearing old garments and poor in technology understood the great privilege of being children of the Giver of Life.

Truth has always been present and never faltered when facing the mundane arguments that the powerful and the vast majority of people used to justify their habits and their laws. Their alleged teachings only served to shatter the conscience and create a false sense of peace that was sustained by the belief that their paths of violence and oppression were endorsed by God.

TRUE PROPHETS

Men declared war on the truth when they blindly decided to follow the deceitful words of those religious leaders who, while sowing impiety, introduced dark teachings that stained the name of the Creator for millennia. The losers were the men of yesterday and of today who willingly surrendered their souls to norms and stories that instill in us the most disgusting indifference and, in the worst of cases, make us murderers. We could not recognize the deception because of the hardness of our hearts, and with our eyes closed, we wanted to justify and defend those stories that attribute the most atrocious acts to instructions allegedly dictated by God.

If a man does not have a sensible heart that is able to recognize the darkness in front of him, how could he ever expect to see anything at all? Due to that lack of sensibility, the people accepted and emulated the cruelest behaviors merely because the writings claimed that they were decrees of the Creator, as it was in the cases narrated in Joshua 7:15-25, in which a man and his family were stoned to death supposedly to calm the wrath of God; Deuteronomy 13:6-10, which says: "thou shalt not consent unto him, nor hearken unto him; neither shall thine eye spare him, neither shalt thou pity him...but thou shalt in any case kill him"; or Leviticus 24:11-23, where a man is stoned by the whole congregation for having cursed the name of God, an example that afterward would be used to turn impiety into a norm and forgiveness into a crime, becoming the justification to murder anyone who questioned the ancient traditions. In this manner, the impious were exalted by the people, who with their indifference ignored the great value of mercy and never found the use for forgiveness.

But the truth found shelter in Micah, who said to the people: "He hath shewn thee, O man, what is good: and what doth Jehovah require of thee, but to do justly, and to love goodness, and to walk humbly with thy God?" (Micah 6:8). Similarly, Zechariah also provided shelter for the truth by declaring: "Thus speaketh Jehovah of hosts, saying, execute true judgment, and shew loving-kindness and mercies one to another, and oppress not the widow and the fatherless, the stranger and the afflicted; and let none of you imagine evil against his brother in your heart" (Zechariah 7:9-10). And the true Ezekiel showed them the nature of God by declaring in his name: "And the wicked, if he turn from all his sins which he hath committed, and keep all my statutes, and do judgment and justice, he shall certainly live, he shall not die. None of his transgressions which he hath committed shall be remembered against him; in his righteousness which he hath done shall he live" (Ezekiel 18:21-22).

The purpose behind the creation is for the soul of man to learn and grow, moving from darkness to understanding to make way for his spirit.

To what purpose is the death penalty other than to quench the thirst for revenge? And to what use is revenge but to intoxicate reason and to blind the spirit? What is the purpose of paying death with death, destruction with more destruction? What good does it serve a punishment that annihilates the life that we should be reforming? We all are born innocent, but nobody is born being holy. The creation is the opportunity that has been given to all of us to reach understanding and become fully aware of our own existence. If even the wisest of men need many years of reflection to reach understanding, why do we insist on cutting short the lives of those ones who need more time to understand? This universe has just one Creator, and He chose life; man does not have the right to destroy what he will never be able to create. Only a man who is not entirely aware of his own existence is capable of snatching the life of another.

Just as oppression and indifference cannot stand before the piercing words of the true prophets, in that same way, all other falsehoods will be torn down by the sound judgment and sensibility of the truth, which can also be found in the words of a child or in the silence of reflection. The truth strips bare the arrogant man's

TRUE PROPHETS

self-pride, astonishes the wise and empowers the meek. The more deceptive the argument, the sharper the truth against it; its consistency outlives all the contradictions of men and the righteous will always protect it, not out of pride or love for controversy but for the sake of humanity.

When man uses his most skillful eloquence to try to justify the accumulation of wealth, or his most sublime arguments to establish idolatry, or resorts to his most seductive stories to drown himself in his own debaucheries, the truth is able to sustain itself with the simple, transparent objectivity that comes from detachment. Man commits a terrible error when he believes himself incapable of understanding the truth or, even worse, when he thinks the truth has no logical explanation, and he intends to live until the end of his days according to blind faith.

Man was created to reach understanding, and reality exists only to be understood. That is a debt we owe to all those men and women who risked their lives again and again for the sake of defending the truth and challenged entire nations with nothing more than wise, sharp-edged words. All for the noble reason of leaving a legacy for other generations.

When the voice of creation penetrates the deepest confines of the human soul, it does so because the truth has finally managed to find a resting place in a man whose sensibility has allowed him to recognize its beauty.

The fig tree is shaken

Around the year 600 BC, the Kingdom of Judah was under the threat of Babylonian invasion. Isaiah, Amos and Hosea had already left their legacy, while Jeremiah and Zephaniah started forging theirs during and despite the reign of King Josiah. Years later, they would pass the torch to Ezekiel—not to be confused with the scribe responsible for the last nine chapters of the book of Ezekiel—. Their writings were capable of overthrowing the demons that enslave the soul, but for reasons that will be discussed in another chapter, this did not occur and, although some people decided to live according to their wise words, society as a whole preferred to follow the false prophets and all their teachings.

Despite the outcry of the true prophets, despite their wise words and blameless example, the hardness of heart became the pride of the people, and violence became their god as they found their justification in ancient writings that exalted arrogance and intolerance. The merciful were seen as weak men, the meek were considered fools and those who had self-control were judged as if they were possessed by a demon. The straight paths were despised, and to the truth they shouted: "Heresy, heresy!"

Jerusalem, the impressive and vibrant city, continued to be a celebration of oppression, a slaughterhouse that, with its laws, destroyed both body and soul. A kingdom whose king was terror itself and its subjects fed on apathy. But there is only one fate for the cities that are built with violence and sustained with oppression. When the people decided to ignore the words of prudence, love and self-control spoken by the true prophets, they sealed their destiny. The teachings of the true Jews were sincere warnings and instructions. However, the people were not satisfied with just ignoring them, but they persecuted them, humiliated them and sometimes even killed them.

In spite of this, the fate that would befall Jerusalem at the hands of Babylon was not due to divine resentment; God is not a man, that He should be thirsty for revenge. When the prophets personify the wrath of God, they do so metaphorically. The destruction of Jerusalem and the captivity of its leaders would be the result of a simple law of existence: when an organism sustains itself by destroying or oppressing others, it inevitably generates so much tension around itself that, sooner or later, everything else turns against it. When oppression and lies persist among men, and their leaders believe in pride and arms rather than in peace and self-sacrifice, they bring destruction upon their heads.

Ezekiel's writings describe the years just before the exile to Babylon by saying: "Make the chain; for the land is full of bloody crimes, and the city is full of violence. Therefore will I bring the worst of the nations, and they shall possess their houses; and I will make the pride of the strong to cease; and their sanctuaries shall be profaned" (Ezekiel 7:23-24).

The Babylonian Empire was advancing towards Jerusalem, and there was no army that could stop it. By the year 589 BC, the great city would be surrounded by the Babylonian army for the second time, on this occasion with a more definitive purpose:

> *And I saw when it opened the sixth seal, and there was a great earthquake; and the sun became black as hair sackcloth, and the whole moon became as blood, and the stars of heaven fell upon the earth, as a fig tree, shaken by a great wind, casts its unseasonable figs. And the heaven was removed as a book rolled up, and every mountain and island were removed out of their places. And the kings of the earth, and the great, and the chiliarchs, and the rich, and the strong, and every bondman and freeman, hid themselves in the caves and in the rocks of the mountains. (Revelation 6:12-15)*

With that description, the Book of Revelation refers to the moment when the Babylonian Empire, under the command of Nebuchadnezzar, destroys Jerusalem and takes captive its main leaders and other Jews who could be useful for the empire. That is why the author of Revelation, just a few lines before, in verse 8 of the same chapter, speaks about the same four calamities—sword, famine, pestilence and beasts—that are mentioned in Ezekiel 14:21-22 when describing the times of the exile and the destruction of Jerusalem.

WHEN THE THUNDERS SPEAK

The fig tree was shaken violently and, in that manner, ended the years of oppression that had been instituted by its leaders, most of whom were taken captive to Babylon. But the land of Judah was not destroyed completely. There remained a poor and humble remnant of the people whose souls would finally have a rest from the spiritual and political yoke to which they were subjected by the priests and their false prophets.

"And after this I saw four angels standing upon the four corners of the earth, holding fast the four winds of the earth, that no wind might blow upon the earth, nor upon the sea, nor upon any tree" (Revelation 7:1). When their rulers were exiled to Babylon, the people of Judah enjoyed a time of peace in which they were not disturbed by the empires that surrounded them.

Later, in 539 BC, Persia, the mighty empire of the east, invaded Babylon. King Cyrus of Persia freed the leaders of Judah who were exiled to Babylon and encouraged their return to their native land. For that reason, Cyrus—the king of the empire from the rising sun—is seen by the Jews as a deliverer from the east, a messenger from whom Judah received a second chance:

> And I saw another angel ascending from the sunrising, having the seal of the living God; and he cried with a loud voice to the four angels to whom it had been given to hurt the earth and the sea, saying, Hurt not the earth, nor the sea, nor the trees, until we shall have sealed the bondmen of our God upon their foreheads. (Revelation 7:2-3)

The fig tree was shaken but not cut off. Decades later, it would reestablish its ways of oppression and confusion with branches that would extend to our times. The fig tree would grow so much and get so well embedded into the ground that only one person would be able to uproot it.

TRUE PROPHETS

A sowing field

Gradually, the Kingdom of Judah would begin to grow again, taking as a starting point that second chance brought about by King Cyrus of Persia. In the years to come, the Kingdom of Judah would manage to preserve its identity as a nation despite being involved in innumerable conflicts with the prevailing empires that had been established at its four cardinal points: having Persia to the east; Greece to the west; with the fall of the Greek Empire, the Ptolemaic Kingdom would later form in the south, having its capital in Egypt; while the north would be ruled by the Seleucid Empire, based in Syria, also emerging from the division of the Greek Empire.

Being situated right in the middle of these four empires was like finding yourself in the center of a permanent storm. But the Kingdom of Judah managed to survive as a nation for more than five centuries, and it became a sowing field in which a humble but very wise group of people coexisted with unrighteous men and their unjust laws; quite consistent with the parable that Jesus would use centuries later, in Mathew 13:24-30, when he says that it is necessary to let the darnel and the wheat grow together until the time of harvest. Judah, like creation in general, was a sowing field, and as such, it needed time to bear fruit. "And I heard the number of the sealed, a hundred [and] forty-four thousand, sealed out of every tribe of [the] sons of Israel" (Revelation 7:4).

The 144,000 people represent the good fruits; communities that generation after generation had to live in the shadows because they did not agree with the traditions and the vain laws of the rulers and the rest of the people. These communities of humble men and women preached by example and jealously guarded the writings of the true prophets that were passed down from one group to another, always alert because of the persecutions they could face.

In this fashion, the teachings of the true prophets were transmitted from generation to generation, for more than five centuries, until the arrival of John the Baptist, who had to preach in the desert, on the outskirts of the city, perhaps because in Jerusalem he could easily raise suspicion among the priests who felt threatened by his teachings.

Twelve generations had passed from the time they started rebuilding Jerusalem to the seventh seal. Although people lived in the midst of great violence and deception during all those years, the communities of righteous men and women did not fail in their duty of protecting the legacy of the true prophets. Thanks to their efforts, when the time came, their descendants were able to understand the words of truth spoken to them. And later, when a long-awaited teacher approached them, they would recognize him and shout: "Hosanna, blessed is he who comes in the name of the Lord!"

7

LOCUSTS DOMINION

Locusts over the earth

With the opening of the seventh seal came seven angels who were prepared to sound seven trumpets, each one followed by mysterious events that actually represent immediate circumstances that had an effect on the spiritual state of men. The first six trumpets brought along symbols that embodied the false doctrines that governed the people before the ministry of Jesus, whose impact is underlined by the sounding of the seventh trumpet that occurs within the seventh seal; thus, establishing the truth that would dismantle the deceitfulness of the doctrines of antiquity.

However, even after the example that Jesus himself left nailed to the cross, the false doctrines that had been established since ancient times continued to govern the life of most men. Going against the flow represented an enormous danger to the physical integrity of those who had the courage to do so, but standing idle meant being complicit with an insatiable deception that was hindering the spiritual growth of entire generations. In order to warn people about the lies behind those false teachings, the author of Revelation reveals the deception by using the symbols shown within the first six trumpets, emphasizing the fifth and sixth trumpets, where he uses even clearer words to refer to powerful creatures whose great authority is derived from those false doctrines.

The Book of Revelation goes to great lengths when describing the creatures of the fifth and sixth trumpet because most people continued to be influenced by them, both in a mundane and spiritual way. Thus, it was vital to alert the followers of the truth so they would be able to escape a deception that had been instituted since ancient times. A trickery so well-orchestrated that even today, it defines our behaviors and customs.

For that reason, we will only make a brief explanation of the first four trumpets, with the intention of focusing all our attention on the fifth and sixth trumpets, whose significance will both clarify the meaning of the previous trumpets and establish a point of reference that will help us unveil the message hidden in the rest of the letter:

> *And the first sounded his trumpet: and there was hail and fire, mingled with blood, and they were cast upon the earth; and the third part of the earth was burnt up, and the third part of the trees was burnt up, and all green grass was burnt up. And the second angel sounded his trumpet: and as a great mountain burning with fire was cast into the sea, and the third part of the sea became blood; and the third part of the creatures which were in the sea which had life died; and the third part of the ships were destroyed. And the third angel sounded his trumpet: and there fell out of the heaven a great star, burning as a torch, and it fell upon the third part of the rivers, and upon the fountains of waters. And the name of the star is called Wormwood; and the third part of the waters became wormwood, and many of the men died of the waters because they were made bitter. And the fourth angel sounded his trumpet: and the third part of the sun was smitten, and the third part of the moon, and the third part of the stars; so that the third part of them should be darkened,*

and that the day should not appear for the third part of it, and the night the same. (Revelation 8:7-12)

In order to comprehend those words, we must first understand the relevance false prophets have had since antiquity and be familiar with the way in which they had been described by Jesus. This is illustrated in chapter 7 of the Gospel of Mathew, where Jesus likens false prophets to fruitless trees that are thrown into the fire: "But beware of false prophets, which come to you in sheep's clothing, but within are ravening wolves. By their fruits ye shall know them...So every good tree produces good fruits, but the worthless tree produces bad fruits. Every tree not producing good fruit is cut down and cast into the fire."

Who were the false prophets that Jesus was referring to? For almost two thousand years, we have not given due importance to the many warnings given by Jesus about these false prophets; on the contrary, without realizing it, we have exalted them and considered them honorable and good examples to follow. Even in our times, perhaps out of convenience, we have not wanted to identify who these false prophets are, even though there are enough clues to identify them just by looking at their fruits. A good fruit is not measured by the number of followers but by their spiritual progress and the level of consciousness that they actually demonstrate. The vain prophet who preaches arrogance and selfishness will in effect have more followers than the man who preaches humility and sacrifice; for we prefer leaders who are like us in order to justify our own weaknesses and despise and condemn those who seek to reform our evil habits.

People from that time period, just like us today, blindly followed and exalted those men who were venerated as prophets without questioning their actions and norms, not even to the slightest extent, no matter how obscure they may have been. Men who in their long speeches ordered to unleash a sea of violence again and again while mentioning a few words of mercy to disguise themselves as sheep. But the blood that still drips from their fangs is obvious to those who decide to seek the truth. Nonetheless, even though their words smell like vanity, arrogance and idolatry, men continue to cope with the stench of their doctrines because by defending the imperfections of these false prophets, they also defend themselves.

The grass that is thrown into the fire represents those who followed the false doctrines of men. Comparing people to the grass of the field was not a strange concept. This similitude is made more than ten times in the writings that make up the Bible. To cite some examples, the book of Isaiah says: "All flesh is grass, and all the comeliness thereof as the flower of the field. The grass withereth, the flower fadeth, for the breath of Jehovah bloweth upon it: surely the people is grass" (Isaiah 40:6-7); and the First Epistle of Peter, chapter 1, repeats the same concept.

Whereas the first trumpet warns people about false prophets, the three trumpets that follow refer to the corruption that befell three sets of ancient writings, which in turn caused great harm to the spiritual progress of men. Later on, we will talk in more detail about that subject and the meaning behind the symbols of the "sea," the "springs of waters," and the "celestial objects"; in the meantime, we will limit ourselves to noting that the trumpets are giving us a warning that one-third of them had been altered, thus corrupting their essence: a burning mountain turned one-third of the sea into blood; the star known as wormwood made bitter one-third of the springs of waters; and one-third of the celestial bodies were darkened.

As we go further into the central message of the Book of Revelation, it will become more obvious what is the true meaning of the sea, the springs of waters, and the celestial objects, and the face of the false prophet will become more recognizable, but for now it is necessary to focus on the sounding of the fifth and sixth trumpets:

> *And the fifth angel sounded [his] trumpet: and I saw a star out of the heaven fallen to the earth; and there was given to it the key of the pit of the abyss. And it opened the pit of the abyss; and there went up smoke out of the pit as [the] smoke of a great furnace; and the sun and the air were darkened with the smoke of the pit. And out of the smoke came forth locusts on the earth, and power was given to them as the scorpions of the earth have power; and it was said to them, that they should not injure the grass of the earth, nor any green thing, nor any tree, but the men who have not the seal of God on their foreheads: and it was given to them that they should not kill them, but that they should be tormented five months; and their torment [was] as [the] torment of a scorpion when it strikes a man. And in those days shall men seek death, and shall in no way find it; and shall desire to die, and death flees from them. And the likenesses of the locusts [were] like to horses prepared for war; and upon their heads as crowns like gold, and their faces as faces of men; and they had hair as women's hair, and their teeth were as of lions, and they had breastplates as breastplates of iron, and the sound of their wings [was] as the sound of chariots of many horses running to war; and they have tails like scorpions, and stings; and their power [was] in their tails to hurt men five months. (Revelation 9:1-10)*

All of the aforementioned features are common traits of certain figures who were given dominion and power over the Jewish people for many generations. The Jews who opposed the authority of these locusts lost their lives or were condemned to exile; however, the rest of men who voluntarily became disciples of these figures ended up losing even more, as the deception made them accept a state of spiritual blindness that extended beyond death.

WHEN THE THUNDERS SPEAK

Several centuries later, the same poison of those peculiar figures would condemn Jesus to the stake with the consent of the majority of the people. And although these locusts with tails of scorpions have been spreading their poison since ancient times, there have always been righteous Jews who opposed their laws, and on numerous occasions the writings of the true prophets are proof of that.

To determine who or what the locusts are, it is necessary to identify which character complies with each of the nine symbolic traits the author of Revelation uses to describe them.

According to the author of Revelation, the locusts are known for the following:

1. They were given authority.
2. They tormented men five months.
3. The rumble of their wings was like the noise of chariots of horses going to battle.
4. On their heads, they wore something like crowns of gold.
5. Their faces were like human faces.
6. They had hair like women's hair.
7. They had breastplates similar to iron breastplates.
8. Their teeth were like those of lions.
9. They had tails similar to scorpions and had stings in their tails.
10. Their king was Apollyon (which means "destroyer" in Greek).

Within the Bible itself, there are clear clues about certain figures whose profiles fit with each and every one of the characteristics mentioned in Revelation concerning the locusts.

The first trait, that of having power, is obvious. You just have to be slightly familiar with the Bible to know about the great authority the high priests exercised over the Jewish people since the founding of the first Kingdom of Israel until the destruction of the second temple. That is, they still had authority during the first half of the first century, even when Judea was under the control of the Roman Empire. Their authority was based on religious laws, but their influence extended to political and judicial matters, and, in many instances, they even performed the role of the king.

Torment men five months

The second characteristic of the locusts is having the authority to torment men five months. These months corresponded to specific dates in which the high priests had the power to force all men to perform rituals and carry out the machinations of their religious leaders. Certainly, the authority of the locusts was much greater and overwhelming during those five months of the year.

During those five months, the five major solemn feasts of the Temple took place, and these periodic events gave the locusts an enormous convening power to gather all the men of Judea in one single place, the city of Jerusalem. Although these solemn feasts were considered sacred by most people, many Jews were aware of the vain and idolatrous nature of those events because instead of encouraging good deeds, such traditions only served to saturate the soil with the great amount of blood that had to be spilled to satisfy the insatiable appetite of the altar. For many people, traditions turn into sacred feasts they are willing to defend with their own lives; for the rulers, they become a precious tool to manipulate the people; but for the truth, a tradition that does not soften the heart of man nor build up his character is a repetitive vanity that over time blunts his mind.

These solemn feasts were openly criticized by some renowned Jews from antiquity. One of the most controversial cases can be found within the book of Isaiah, which in its first chapter says: "Hear the word of Jehovah... wickedness and the solemn meeting I cannot bear. Your new moons and your set feasts my soul hateth: they are a burden to me; I am wearied of bearing them." While in chapter 5 of the book of Amos, it is written:

> *Thus said Jehovah...I hate, I despise your feasts, and I will not smell a sweet odour in your solemn assemblies. For if ye offer up unto me burnt-offerings and your oblations, I will not accept them; neither will I regard the peace-offerings of your fatted beasts...but let judgment roll down as waters, and righteousness as an ever-flowing stream. (Amos 5:21-24)*

During five months of the year, however, large crowds gathered around the temple to commemorate the main solemn feasts and offer the corresponding sacrifices. The Old Testament talks in great detail about these major feasts and how they were distributed throughout five different months: the Jewish months of Nisan, Iyar, Sivan, Tishrei and Kislev.

1. Nisan: during the first month of the Jewish ecclesiastical calendar, the month of Nisan, according to chapter 9 of the Book of Numbers and twelve of Exodus, it was mandatory for all Jewish men to be present in Jerusalem to celebrate the Passover (Pesach) in the 14th day, which was immediately followed by the feast of seven days of Unleavened Bread (Hag-Ha-Matzah), also celebrated during the same month.
2. Iyar: according to Numbers 9:11, during the second ecclesiastical month, the Second Passover was celebrated, which was established for the Jews who could not attend the first.
3. Sivan: according to Numbers 28:26, Leviticus 23:15-16 and Deuteronomy 16:9-12, the feast of Pentecost (Shavuot) occurred seven weeks after the first Passover, that is, in the third Jewish month, Sivan.

4. Tishrei: in the seventh month of the ecclesiastical calendar, the feast of Tabernacles (Sukkoth) was held, which consisted of eight days and culminated with the celebration of a solemn assembly, as stated in Leviticus 23:36. During the same month, the celebration of the Trumpets (Rosh HaShanah) and the Day of Atonement (Yom Kippur) were also observed.
5. Kislev: as reported by the first Book of Maccabees 4:59, the Feast of Dedication, also known as Hanukkah or Feast of Lights, was held in the Temple of Jerusalem during the ninth ecclesiastical month, Kislev. Although this solemn feast was instituted many years after the others, it was of great importance for many Jews, and for the priests in particular, because it commemorates the occasion in which the altar was reconsecrated after recovering the Temple of Jerusalem from the hands of King Antiochus IV of the Seleucid Empire. John 10:22 serves as evidence to confirm that this feast was still celebrated in Jerusalem even during the first century.

The festival of Purim cannot be taken into account because it did not belong to the temple festivals of Jerusalem. It had originated in Persia instead, according to the Book of Esther, and it was celebrated by the Jews in exile, not by the Jewish priests of the temple.

On the other hand, the solemn feasts that took place during the five months mentioned earlier were directly related to the Temple of Jerusalem, and the locusts took advantage of them to consolidate their authority over the entire Jewish people

Figure 1 illustrates the five months during which a large number of men were obliged to visit the temple.

Figure 1. Torment men five months

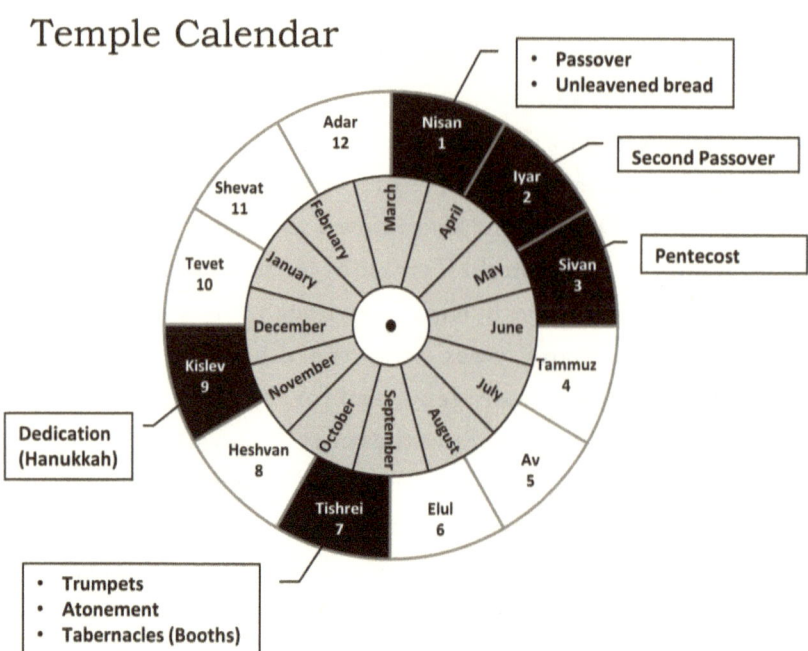

Note: the festival of Purim is not included because it was established in Persia, by the Jewish diaspora, and it did not belong to the solemn feasts of the Temple of Jerusalem.

A great amount of power was concentrated in Jerusalem during those five months, especially because it was a time when modern means of communications did not exist. Consequently, the agglomeration of a large number of people served as the perfect scenario to transmit and execute the objectives of the locusts. In addition to carrying out the offerings and rituals, these crowds served to coordinate battles, to condemn the enemies of the priests' doctrine, to collect resources and to reaffirm the laws of the temple—all in one place, five months each year.

LOCUSTS DOMINION

The appearance of the locusts

In a brilliant way, the author of Revelation describes the locusts with images and symbols that reveal their identity while keeping the true meaning of his words hidden from the eyes of those who could start a religious persecution against the author and his letter.

Revelation 9:7-10 describes the appearance of the locusts. As mentioned before, they had golden crowns, their faces look like human faces, their hair was like women's hair, their teeth were like those of a lion, they had breastplates, the sound of their wings was like the sound of horse-drawn chariots running to war, and they had tails like scorpions.

The garments of the high priest of the Temple of Jerusalem were, according to the eyes of men and their concept of beauty, splendid and distinguished him from the rest of the people who also worked in the temple. The high priest's garments are described in detail in chapter 28 of the Book of Exodus, where we can begin to see clearly the physical appearance of the locusts.

We will start with the most obvious feature of the locusts, the golden crown. The Book of Exodus specifies that the high priest, who at that time was Aaron, had to wear a golden crown on his forehead above the turban (miter).

> *And thou shalt make a thin plate of pure gold, and engrave on it, as the engravings of a seal, Holiness to Jehovah! And thou shalt put it on a lace of blue, and it shall be upon the turban—upon the front of the turban shall it be. And it shall be upon Aaron's forehead. (Exodus 28:36-38)*

Revelation also specifies that the locusts have faces like men's faces and hair similar to women's hair. It is not necessary to stress the fact that they have faces of men, but as for the phrase "hair as woman's hair," we can refer to the instructions given in ancient writings relating to the physical appearance of the high priests. In Leviticus 21:10, the high priests are commanded to cover their heads: "And the high priest among his brethren, on whose head the anointing oil was poured, and who is consecrated to put on the garments, shall not uncover his head..." This puts them in the same situation as the women of Judea, who had to cover their hair according to the customs of the people. Ancient writings illustrate the fact that women from that period of time used to cover their heads. The Bible, for example, in Numbers 5:18, specifies that the priest has to "uncover the head" of women to perform one of the rites related to jealousy or infidelity; while the Jewish Talmud, in Ketuboth 72, also attests to the Jewish women's habit of covering their heads. In that sense, the ordinance that stated that the high priest could not uncover his head is similar to the custom of Jewish women from that time, who were required to keep their heads covered in public places.

Another feature of the locusts is that they had breastplates similar to breastplates of iron. In Exodus 28:15-19, the famous breastplate of judgment is described among the items that make up the garments of the high priest. It was square in shape and carried twelve different stones arranged in four rows of three stones each. Each stone was engraved with the name of one of the tribes of Israel. According to the words of the first-century Jewish historian Flavius Josephus (Antiquities of the Jews, book 3, chapter 8, paragraph 9), the high priest's breastplate of judgment "shone with splendor" just before the people began to march to a battle.

As the author of Revelation proceeds with the description of the locusts, he says that "the sound of their wings was as the sound of chariots of many horses running to war." In this case, the author is not talking about a visual element but some type of noise. As in the previous cases, we can find the explanation for this strange description in the Book of Exodus. Another peculiarity of the garments of the high priest consisted in hanging many little bells all around the skirts of the cloak: "a golden bell and a pomegranate, a golden bell and a pomegranate, in the skirts of the cloak round about" (Exodus 28:34).

Those bells that hung from the cloak of the high priest produced a loud and distinctive sound every time he walked. In the same manner, hanging bells to horses was a common practice in ancient times; there are numerous examples in literature, folklore and even in films that illustrate the particular sound made by horse chariots from antiquity. It is easy to understand that every time the high priest moved, the bells that hung from his cloak made a noise that was very similar to the sound made by the bells mounted on chariots of horses. The analogy used by the author of Revelation could not be better; you just have to close your eyes and visualize the high priest moving around the temple with the border of his cloak full of bells making a constant and distinctive noise.

Figure 2 shows the peculiar garments of the high priest, which resemble the description given to us by the author of Revelation.

Figure 2. Garments of the High Priest

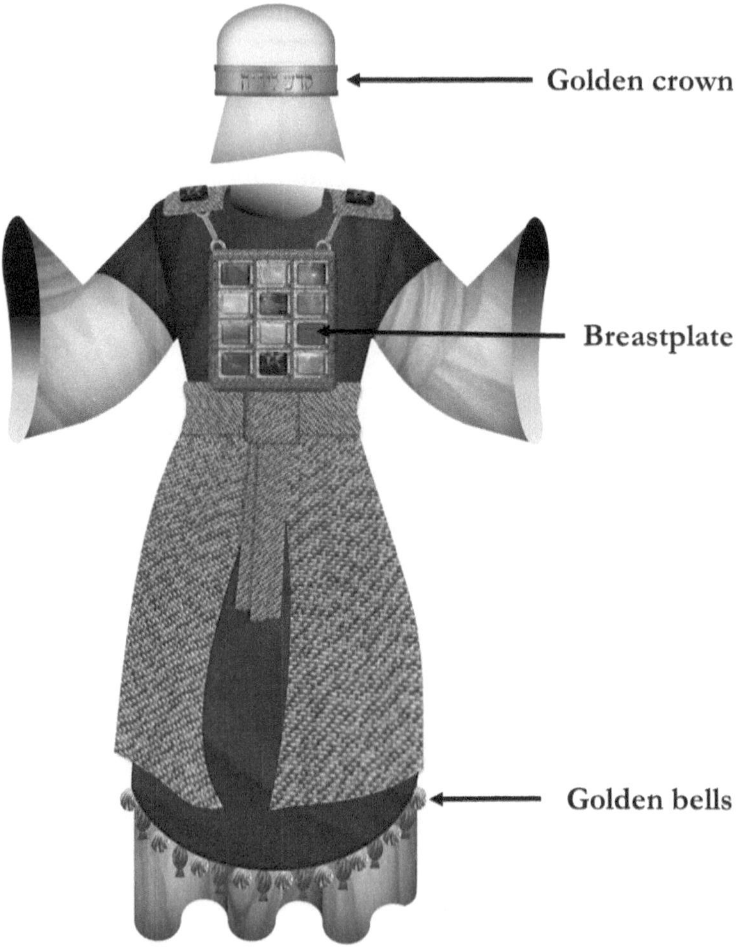

- Golden crown
- Breastplate
- Golden bells

While the above features serve to clarify the identity of the locusts according to their physical appearance, the mysterious phrases "teeth as teeth of lions" and "tails like scorpions" reveal their nature, their dark and deceptive ways.

LOCUSTS DOMINION

Knowing that his readers were familiar with the sayings of the true prophets, the author of Revelation uses similar analogies with the intention of allowing those who are acquainted with these writings to discover the identity of the locusts. Since ancient times, the true prophets always used their wise words to unmask the deception that their rulers articulated to manipulate people.

> *And Jehovah will cut off from Israel head and tail, palm-branch and rush, in one day: the ancient and honourable, he is the head; and the prophet that teacheth lies, he is the tail. For the guides of this people mislead them. (Isaiah 9:14-16)*

The words of Isaiah refer to the permanent collusion that existed between the leaders of Israel, where the rulers—the head—and the false prophets—the tail—backed each other to keep the people deceived.

In that same manner, Revelation describes the locusts as creatures that have a tail with stings. Just as the tails of scorpions are deceptive and full of venom, so are the locusts that maintain their power and subdue their victims by colluding with the false prophets. If previously they were able to consolidate their power thanks to the false prophets' lies, now they did it through their writings, which endorsed all their laws and their ways of living.

Both figures, the high priest and the false prophet, presented themselves before the people as if they were institutions independent of one another. By showing mutual agreement, they created the false perception that their decisions were endorsed by God Himself, thus perpetuating the scam. In that way, no matter how obscure their intentions were, their decisions ended up being indisputable. For hundreds of years, the political-religious system that dominated the region was based on the complicity that existed between its leaders.

WHEN THE THUNDERS SPEAK

The high priest was the head, and the false prophet was his tail; the high priest spoke, and the false prophet approved his words; the high priest devoured, and the false prophet praised him; the high priest condemned to death, and the false prophet ratified the sentence: before with his voice, now with his writings.

Revelation also states that the locusts have teeth like teeth of lions. Concerning this phrase, we also find answers in the writings of the true prophets, who liken the rulers of the people to lions.

"There is a conspiracy of her prophets in the midst of her like a roaring lion ravening the prey; they devour souls; they take away treasure and precious things; they increase her widows in the midst of her; her priests do violence to my law" (Ezekiel 22:25-26). Zephaniah also makes similar comparisons when talking about the rulers: "Her princes in the midst of her are roaring lions; her judges are evening wolves, that leave nothing for the morning" (Zephaniah 3:3). And Micah likened them to predators:

> *And I said, Hear, I pray you, ye heads of Jacob, and princes of the house of Israel: Is it not for you to know judgment? Ye who hate the good, and love evil; who pluck off their skin from them, and their flesh from off their bones; and who eat the flesh of my people, and flay their skin from off them, and break their bones, and chop them in pieces as for the pot, and as flesh within the cauldron. (Micah 3:1-3)*

For righteous men, the deception of their rulers was obvious. And although for most of the people the high priest was seen as the most sublime man on earth, for the true prophets, they were nothing more than predators, savage beasts who devoured the flesh of the people with their cruel laws and their vile actions. No matter how sumptuous their appearance was, their sharp and vulgar fangs were visible to everyone whenever they opened their mouths to enact unjust and cruel laws.

LOCUSTS DOMINION

"They have a king over them, the angel of the abyss: his name in Hebrew, Abaddon, and in Greek he has for name Apollyon. The first woe has passed. Behold, there come yet two woes after these things" (Revelation 9:11-12).

Ἀπολλύων (Apollyon) is a Greek word meaning "destroyer," which is the active participle of ἀπόλλυμι (apóllymi), a verb whose meaning is "to destroy, kill or condemn to death." Most of the time, when that verb appears in the writings of the New Testament, it is used to refer to killing or destroying lives. On many occasions, it is even the term used by priests and Pharisees when they spoke of condemning Jesus to death, as is the case in Matthew 27:20, Mark 3:6 and Luke 19:47, among others.

It is important to remember that the first persecutions against Christians were not undertaken by the Roman Empire but by the priests of the temple in Jerusalem, who saw the teachings of Jesus as a clear affront to their writings and traditions. Beginning with the machinations of the High Priest Caiaphas that culminated in the execution of Jesus; later, another high priest would begin the interrogation that would lead to the stoning of Stephen, according to Acts 7:1; then, in the same book, chapter 5 verses 27 to 33, the writing talks about the intention of the high priest and the Sanhedrin to kill Peter and other apostles; and later, in chapter 25, it mentions the desire of the high priest to assassinate Paul; while the writings of the Jewish historian Flavius Josephus describe how James the Just was stoned after the high priest Ananias ben Ananias formulated an accusation against him.

In the midst of constant threats and persecution that often ended in death sentences, the first Christians would understand perfectly what the author of Revelation was referring to when he said that the locusts had as king over them the "destroyer." With that terminology, they would begin to understand the clues that the author left for them in the letter, whose intention was to let them know that they were on the right path even though they were repudiated by everyone at that moment, especially by the religious leaders of their own people. As expected, many came to doubt the teachings of Jesus after witnessing how a figure as emblematic and honorable as the high priest opposed his words and condemned to death his followers with the only purpose of eradicating the doctrine.

Certainly, the locusts—the high priests of the Temple of Jerusalem—exercised great authority for many centuries and came to influence our current way of thinking more than we can imagine. However, their power and scope could never be compared with that of the second beast, the so-called false prophet.

Breastplates of fire, jacinth and sulfur

With the sixth trumpet, four angels that were bound at the Euphrates River were let loose in order to kill the third part of men, and along with them appeared horsemen with armors of fire, jacinth and sulfur.

There is a historical place located right along the path of the Euphrates River, from which, in fact, well-known figures were released wearing a thick belt wrapped around their chest with the colors of fire, jacinth and sulfur.

The place from which those figures were released is well known to all. The notorious city of Babylon was built in such a way that the Euphrates River cut right through the center. When the city fell to the Persian Empire, important and influential figures who were held captive in Babylon were set free and departed towards Judah. Not only were they allowed to leave Babylon, but they were also given the authority to kill anyone who opposed them: "Also I have given order that whosoever shall alter this rescript, let timber be pulled down from his house, and being set up, let him be hanged thereon" (Ezra 6:11).

LOCUSTS DOMINION

As for the mysterious breastplates of fire, jacinth and sulfur, many translations have made the mistake of adding the word yellow next to, or in substitution of, the word sulfur, which is an understandable mistake because that is the color of such material at ambient temperature; however, in this case, we are talking about burning sulfur, which becomes evident when in the next verse, the author mentions the three words "fire, smoke and sulfur" all together. The implications are interesting and revealing because when sulfur is burning, its appearance changes and takes on a spectacular blue color. Thus, the colors of the breastplates are fire, jacinth and blue.

The Book of Exodus describes a very unique belt that is wrapped around the chest and that has exactly those three colors: "and the girdle, of twined byssus, and blue, and purple, and scarlet, of embroidery" (Exodus 39:29). The Bible does not specify at what height along the torso they wore these belts; but the Jewish historian Flavius Josephus, who had the opportunity to see these belts with his own eyes, gave us more information: "girded to the breast a little above the elbows, by a girdle often going round, four fingers broad, but so loosely woven, that you would think it were the skin of a serpent. It is embroidered with flowers of scarlet, and purple, and blue, and fine twined linen" (Antiquities of the Jews, book 3, chapter 7, paragraph 2).

Both the Book of Exodus 39:29 and Josephus (Antiquities of the Jews 3.7.2) are describing the belt of the ordinary priests of Judah. Their belt was different from the high priest's belt, which had gold in addition to the colors mentioned. The ordinary priests wore their belts around their chest, and they contained three colors: scarlet, purple and blue.

This is not a time to be scandalized but to reflect. As we move forward with the message of Revelation, the waters will become clear.

WHEN THE THUNDERS SPEAK

"And the number of the forces of the horsemen is two myriads of myriads, and I heard the number of them" (Revelation 9:16).

Some versions of the Bible say that this army was made of two hundred million people; however, when we analyze this phrase in the Greek New Testament that is based on the Byzantine text-type, also known as the Majority Text, whose criterion is to use the text that is found in most of the surviving manuscripts, we find that the verse only says, "μυριάδες μυριάδων," which means myriads of myriads, that is, a multitude. The word myriad could also mean ten thousand but in cases where it is said, "myriads of myriads," it simply means a large number or a crowd. It is not two hundred million people, not only because that number does not correspond with the Greek Byzantine version but also because it would be impossible to assemble an army of that magnitude, even in modern times.

The author knows the exact number, but he does not specify it openly because providing too much information would pose a major risk; however, by saying, "I heard their number," he implies that it is an exact amount that is known by many. He is referring to the overwhelming number of 4,289 priests, as it is stated in Ezra 2:36-39.

When Babylon fell, 4,289 priests were released. They began their journey towards Judah, which was inhabited by the Jews who had remained in the region, those who had not been taken captive to Babylon and who were mostly humble people. When Nebuchadnezzar invaded Jerusalem more than 70 years before that event, he did not take captive all the Jews; a large number of them remained in Jerusalem and in all of Judah. Those who remained were largely poor people, but they were more sublime than the high priest; many were illiterate but had a more refined knowledge than that of the scribes. They did not perform rites or animal sacrifices, but they offered the most splendid sacrifice of all: mercy and good deeds. Nevertheless, their freedom vanished with the arrival of the locusts and their army with breastplates of red, purple and blue.

Chapter 3 of the Book of Zephaniah, who spoke during the time of King Josiah—that is, before the captivity to Babylon—, after rebuking the princes, judges and priests, says: "And I will leave in the midst of thee an afflicted and poor people, and they shall trust in the name of Jehovah. The remnant of Israel shall not work unrighteousness, nor speak lies; neither shall a deceitful tongue be found in their mouth: but they shall feed and lie down, and none shall make them afraid."

At that time, in Judah, there were also other cultures that lived in harmony with the humble Jews who had remained there. But those who came from Babylon were different. They supposedly belonged to the richest families, the rulers and the priestly lineage. Jerusalem had been destroyed because of them, and because of them, it would be destroyed once more.

The Book of Ezra favors the newcomers from Babylon, which is to be expected, for Ezra, besides being a scribe, was also a priest. But his words reflect the atmosphere of conflict that originated with the arrival of the former captives because the inhabitants of Jerusalem did not agree with the intentions of the newcomers.

The priests who came from Babylon had a purpose in mind, and they would carry it out even if they had to fight against the Jews who were already in Judah. By means of a decree from the Persian King Darius, great authority was granted to the arriving priests over all the inhabitants of Jerusalem. He authorized them to both rebuild the temple and use tribute money to cover all their expenses; it was also instructed to provide them with all the animals they needed for their sacrifices. The king also ordered that anyone who did not follow the stipulations of this decree be executed (Ezra 6:7-13).

What importance could these characters and their authority have? Why talk about something that happened so many years ago?

WHEN THE THUNDERS SPEAK

They are the same stumbling block as always. The smoke that came out of the abyss at that time is the same that today clouds our vision. The true Jews of antiquity knew this and never agreed with the high priest or with his army of ordinary priests, who judged according to the flesh and without mercy; loved great buildings, wealth and power; forced the people to shed blood for their rituals; were responsible for maintaining a system of laws that was extremely cruel and oppressive; and, as if these things were not enough, they kept the soul of men in permanent confusion by claiming that all their vanities and atrocities were the will of the Creator.

Still, fear was never an option for the righteous men who have always confronted the locusts and their army. Zephaniah was not afraid of them when he said: "Priests profane the sanctuary, they do violence to the law" (Zephaniah 3:4). While Hosea, armed with courage, said: "And as troops of robbers lie in wait for a man, so the company of priests murder in the way of Shechem; yea, they commit lewdness" (Hosea 6:9). And admirably, risking his life, Jeremiah dared to utter the strongest words against what was most valued by the priests, saying: "Confide ye not in words of falsehood, saying, Jehovah's temple, Jehovah's temple, Jehovah's temple is this" (Jeremiah 7:4).

Whereas the righteous Isaiah always warned about the hypocrisy of the people, saying: "And the Lord saith, Forasmuch as this people draw near with their mouth, and honour me with their lips, but their heart is removed far from me, and their fear of me is a commandment taught of men..." (Isaiah 29:13). And concerning the leaders of Judah, he said: "My people! they that guide thee mislead thee, and destroy the way of thy paths" (Isaiah 3:13).

In many other instances, the true prophets showed admirable courage when challenging a monster that was incredibly thirsty for the blood of its opponents. But their efforts, although they served to open the eyes of multitudes and awaken the souls of many, were not able to end that deceptive and cruel system because the mountain was immense. With their tails, the locusts would continue to poison entire generations for hundreds of years to come. But those Jews who were righteous and humble did not falter and kept waiting for the moment when someone with great wisdom, courage and detachment would come to confront that enormous mountain.

8

JESUS AGAINST THE FIG TREE

The fruitless temple

Jesus decided to return to that peculiar place. There was no turning back. Depending on the circumstances there, he could end up being the victim of horrors capable of shocking the imagination of the most morbid man; but that did not stop him, he started his journey to fulfill the task his conscience would never allow him to abandon.

The first woe had already passed, causing great indignation among righteous men, debauchery among the wicked and consent among the ignorant. Even the unthinkable had been done to break the immutability of the Creator. Dense and overwhelming was the smoke that continued to emanate from the abyss. Like an impressive volcano that is impossible to destroy, it kept intoxicating multitudes with its false doctrines. Great buildings and sumptuous garments to amaze the worldly eyes of men; oppression and cruelty to maintain their loyalty; abolishment of mercy to allow the massacre of the righteous, and bloody rituals to blot out the cry of their own conscience.

In the midst of so much darkness, not many people were able to distinguish between the virtuous path and deception. The profound differences between the nature of the Creator and the commandments of men cannot be seen when we behave like unconscious beings, always following the majority without reflecting on our own individual actions and beliefs.

That is why Jesus was entrusted with a task that he alone would be able to carry out; thus, he had to return to the place where his life would be in clear danger, but just before arriving, something very interesting and revealing happened. On his way back to that unusual place, he was hungry and approached a fig tree, a tree that is known for its large size and its sweet and popular fruit, but after realizing that it did not have one single fig, he said: "Let no one eat fruit of thee any more for ever" (Mark 11:14). Immediately afterwards, Jesus arrived in Jerusalem and entered the temple to drive out all those who were selling and buying merchandise for the sacrifices, throwing the table of the money-changers and of those who were selling doves.

The episode that had occurred just moments before, between Jesus and the fig tree, was a clear allusion to the Temple of Jerusalem, whose doctrine bore no fruit despite all of its power and centuries of uninterrupted operation.

But Jesus' indignation did not stop there. Not only did he cast out those who were buying and selling animals for the sacrifices, but he "suffered not that any one should carry any package through the temple" (Mark 11:16). That particular phrase is one of the most transcendental and, at the same time, most ignored verses; those words reveal that at that moment, Jesus stopped the entire sacrificial system since in order to perform the rituals at the altar, they needed to carry utensils and vessels to slaughter the animals. According to Mark 11:16, he did not let anyone bring utensils to the temple. With that action, Jesus did the unimaginable. He dared to openly confront the great mountain, an event that by itself was enough to make the fig tree feel threatened as never before. The sacrificial system was the pillar of the doctrine of the temple and one of the main sources

JESUS AGAINST THE FIG TREE

of its wealth. For that reason, what Jesus had just done in front of all the people would become his death sentence. With this act, he defied in public the authority of the overly esteemed priests and discarded their sacred customs.

Even if the most eloquent man came to affirm that those vain sacrifices were instituted by God Himself, supposedly to symbolize the death of Jesus, the truth is that the Giver of Life has never asked for blood, nor can He be bought with the fat of lambs; much less would He be interested in symbolizing His paths of righteousness with violent and vulgar rituals. To what purpose is a ritual if it hardens the heart of man? What truth could there be in an action that teaches you to despise the wonder of life by disrespecting creation? Mercy is worth much more than any symbolism, and the contemplation of creation is more effective at opening the eyes of men than the shedding of innocent blood. He who understands mercy understands its fullness.

After the risky feat Jesus and his followers conducted in the temple, they left the city in the evening. The next day, before returning to Jerusalem, they came across the fig tree once again, and "they saw the fig-tree dried up from the roots. And Peter, remembering what Jesus had said, says to him, 'Rabbi, see, the fig-tree which thou cursed is dried up'" (Mark 11:20-21).

Then, they returned to Jerusalem, and Jesus continued teaching to everyone who came to him. After Jesus answered many questions, a scribe approached him to ask him what was the greatest of the commandments. Jesus responded by saying that the main commandment was to love God above all things, and the second one was to love your neighbor as yourself. Jesus assured the man that "There is not another commandment greater than these." The scribe agrees by replying, "Right, teacher; thou hast spoken according to the truth. For he is one, and there is none other besides him; and to love him with all the heart... and to love one's neighbour as one's self, is more than all the burnt-offerings and sacrifices." Then Jesus says to him, "Thou art not far from the kingdom of God" (Mark 12:32-34).

In such a way, with the authority and wisdom that only truth is able to grant, Jesus continued to answer all the inquiries without fear, knowing that, although the fate of the fruitless fig tree had already been sealed, he would end up being one of its victims.

Seal the things spoken

"And I saw another strong angel coming down out of the heaven, clothed with a cloud, and the rainbow upon his head, and his countenance as the sun, and his feet as pillars of fire" (Revelation 10:1).

We have now reached one of the most important events in the Book of Revelation: the testimony of an extraordinary angel and the sounding of the seventh trumpet.

The description given at the beginning of chapter 10, concerning the strong angel, employs terminology that is often used when referring to Jesus. These words, along with other elements that occur later in the same chapter, confirm that, indeed, the mighty angel whose feet are as pillars of fire is Jesus.

The cloud is a symbol that is used to represent a glorious event, and Matthew 24:30, Luke 21:27 and Revelation 14:14 associate the term with the Son of Man. The rainbow on his head represents the covenant of peace between God, men and all creatures on earth. The meaning behind the rainbow comes from the story of the flood, where at the end of the storm, a rainbow appears, and it is used to symbolize a covenant between the Creator and His creation:

> And I, behold, I establish my covenant with you, and with your seed after you; and with every living soul which is with you, fowl as well as cattle, and all the animals of the earth with you... I set

> *my bow in the clouds, and it shall be for a sign of the covenant between me and the earth. (Genesis 9:9-13)*

Whereas concerning the commanding figure from chapter 1, who looked like the Son of Man and had a sharp two-edged sword, Revelation 1:16 says, "his countenance was as the sun shines in its power." This is similar to Revelation 10:1, which states that the countenance of the strong angel was "as the sun." Later we will look at other elements that confirm the identity of this angel.

> *And [he] cried with a loud voice as a lion roars. And when he cried, the seven thunders uttered their own voices. And when the seven thunders spoke, I was about to write: and I heard a voice out of the heaven saying, Seal the things which the seven thunders have spoken, and write them not. (Revelation 10:3-4)*

Why would the author of Revelation be instructed not to write down what the seven thunders said? What was the outcry of the angel, and what words could be so important and, at the same time, troubling as not to write them? Precisely, John was compelled to write his letter in a coded manner because of what those words implied. Not all ears were prepared to listen to those words; on the contrary, many anxiously expected to be scandalized in order to condemn and destroy writings of this kind.

Jesus' testimony showed the norm by which a righteous man should be measured and cleared the path that leads to understanding. He also testified against all the absurdities of false doctrines, which even to this day continue to be part of our lives because many have failed to grasp Jesus' message in all its fullness.

He did not need an army to dismantle the false doctrine that kept his brothers in chains; his discerning words and his sincere and noble deeds were enough to complete the task. He was a bearer of good news, but he also brought severe criticism, and when he roared like a lion, the seven thunders delivered their verdict.

Every false doctrine falls apart when it is compared to the underlying attributes of a truly conscious being. If all the instructions given to the seven communities mentioned in Revelation were adopted as virtues that must be developed by those who seek the truth, it would not be difficult to unmask any false doctrine. Deceitful teachings, even though they profess a desire to live according to many of the attributes of the Creator, they always end up repudiating at least one of those qualities. The fruitless fig tree is no exception, and its deception is visible to all when the thunders emit their voices.

Revelation 2:19-20 gives us an idea of the qualities that should be essential in a doctrine whose goal is to reach a full understanding of reality and existence: good deeds, love, faith, service, patience, self-control and later works should be greater than the first ones, that is, continuous improvement.

The fruitless fig tree is sterile because its doctrine is based on lording over others, the use of violence to validate its laws, mundane and idolatrous rituals, and boasting of stories about men who did "great signs" and ordered the destruction of entire populations; while meek men that convey brave teachings are despised. All in clear opposition to the qualities that guide us to know the nature of the Creator.

The deception behind the false doctrine was obvious to those who had understood the words of Jesus, but if the author of Revelation had denounced the fruitless fig tree publicly, it would have led to his certain death and the destruction of the letter, so he was instructed to seal what the seven thunders spoke and not to write it openly.

> *But in the days of the voice of the seventh angel, when he is about to sound the trumpet, the mystery of God also shall be completed,*

JESUS AGAINST THE FIG TREE

> *as he has made known the glad tidings to his own bondmen the prophets. (Revelation 10:7)*

Jesus brought about the understanding that many had been waiting for and embodied the culmination of the words of those men who proclaimed that one day the light would take its rightful place and the lies would be exposed. It is a known fact that Jesus' teachings represent a pivotal moment in the lives of billions of people. However, there are still things to be revealed that are as impactful as they are edifying, and the author of Revelation set out to bring them to light.

Two witnesses

"And I went to the angel, saying to him to give me the little book. And he says to me, Take and eat it up: and it shall make thy belly bitter, but in thy mouth it shall be sweet as honey" (Revelation 10:9). Even though Jesus had brought about good news concerning the possibility of true reformation in the lives of men and women, he also spoke of lamentations and prophesied about a time of suffering and calamities for many in Judea.

> *By your patient endurance gain your souls. But when ye see Jerusalem encompassed with armies, then know that its desolation is drawn nigh. Then let those who are in Judaea flee to the mountains, and those who are in the midst of it depart out, and those who are in the country not enter into it; for these are days of avenging, that all the things that are written may be accomplished. But woe to them that are with child and to them who give suck in those days, for there shall be great distress upon the land and wrath upon this people. And they shall fall by the edge of the sword, and be led captive into all the nations; and Jerusalem shall be trodden*

down of the nations until the times of the nations be fulfilled. (Luke 21: 19-24)

With those grim words, Jesus refers to the time when Jerusalem and the temple would be besieged and destroyed, approximately forty years later. That is why he says to the people who were listening to him that "this generation shall in no wise pass away until all come to pass" (Luke 21:32).

In the same way, chapter 11 of Revelation concerns grievous times in Jerusalem and what the book describes as "two witnesses" who warned about it: "And I will give power to my two witnesses, and they shall prophesy a thousand two hundred and sixty days, clothed in sackcloth" (Revelation 11:3).

The Gospel of John, on several occasions, emphasizes the fact that Jesus himself had two witnesses. Such a concept is used to validate his testimony since ancient Jewish law required at least two witnesses in order for a testimony to be accepted as true. "And in your law too it is written that the testimony of two men is true: I am one who bear witness concerning myself, and the Father who has sent me bears witness concerning me" (John 8:17-18). And in the same book, several chapters earlier, it is also written:

> But I have the witness that is greater than that of John; for the works which the Father has given me that I should complete them, the works themselves which I do, bear witness concerning me that the Father has sent me. And the Father who has sent me himself has borne witness concerning me. (John 5:36-37)

The original Greek version of the Book of Revelation reads: "they should prophesy 1,260 days"; that is, the prophecy or the message they carry concerns a time that would last that number of days, which is equivalent to three and a half years. Being dressed in sackcloth was a phrase frequently used when referring to days of mourning and lamentations; which indicates that the prophecy is about grievous times.

Jesus' warnings in Luke 21:19-24 talk about those distressing times, for he advises that "when ye see Jerusalem encompassed with armies, then know that its desolation is drawn nigh. Then let those who are in Judaea flee to the mountains, and those who are in the midst of it depart out." He is referring to the most catastrophic event that had ever happened to Judea: the first rebellion of the Jews against Rome and subsequent outcome. The 1,260 days, equivalent to three and a half years, correspond to the time span starting with the establishment of the radical Jewish government—commanded from Jerusalem—in the winter months of 66 CE until the destruction of Jerusalem by the Romans, which occurred between April and August of 70 CE. That period was marked by frequent battles between radical Jews and Romans as well as by internal violent confrontations between the different factions of the Jewish rebels that were fighting for power.

Those three and a half years are what Jesus was referring to; warning people about the calamities that would befall Jerusalem and all of Judea while having on his side two witnesses: himself and the Father.

For that reason, the original Greek version, when narrating the event in which the two witnesses are killed by the beast, uses the singular form of the word *corpse* (πτῶμα) when referring to their bodies. Revelation 11:8-9 on three occasions mentions the corpses of the two witnesses; in the first two cases, it uses the singular πτῶμα when referring to them, while only in the third instance, it uses the plural πτώματα. The discrepancy occurs in two contiguous verses, which indicates that the author knew the correct way to write the plural of the term. Nevertheless, he decided to use the singular form *corpse* on the first two occasions and not *corpses*.

WHEN THE THUNDERS SPEAK

If we were to make a faithful translation of the original Greek version, verses eight and nine should read as follows: "And their *corpse (πτῶμα)* is in the street of the great city, which spiritually is called Sodom and Egypt, where also our Lord [where their Lord, in the original Greek version] was crucified. And those of the lineages, and of the peoples, and of the tongues, and of the Gentiles see their *corpse* for three and a half days, and they will not allow their corpses to be put in sepulchers."

According to Matthew 27:64, the day after the death of Jesus, the Pharisees and the chief priests asked Pilate to send a Roman guard to watch over the tomb of Jesus for three days. Pilate, who represented the Roman Empire in the province of Judea, granted the request and ordered that the tomb be watched for three days.

The concept of "rising" after three days has always been one of Jesus' hallmarks; however, Revelation is even more specific and says "after three and a half days." This level of detail is often used by writers when there is a need to draw attention to a particular point.

> *And after the three days and a half the spirit of life from God came into them, and they stood upon their feet; and great fear fell upon those beholding them. And I heard a great voice out of the heaven saying to them, Come up here; and they went up to the heaven in the cloud, and their enemies beheld them. (Revelation 11:11-12)*

In this subject, Revelation draws attention to the fact that some parts of the gospels seem to affirm, or have been used to affirm, that the resurrection happened in just one and a half days, dying on Friday afternoon and rising before dawn on Sunday, even though Jesus himself talks about three full days when he mentions the concept of rising on the third day: "For even as Jonas was in the belly of the great fish three days and three nights, thus shall the Son of man be in the heart of the earth three days and three nights" (Matthew 12:40).

JESUS AGAINST THE FIG TREE

But what is even more interesting concerning this subject is that there are Christian writings from the third and fourth century that state that Jesus was arrested on the fourth day of the week, which corresponds to Wednesday—considering that Sunday is the first day of the week—, and that he was crucified on Friday. One of these writings is the *Didascalia Apostolorum*, which states: "And the next day, which was the fourth of the week, He [Jesus] remained in ward in the house of Caiaphas the high priest...And on the next day again, which was the fifth of the week, they brought Him to Pilate the governor. And He remained again in ward with Pilate the night after the fifth day of the week. But when it drew on Friday, they accused Him much...they crucified Him on the same Friday." And the other writing with a similar statement is the *Panarion* by Epiphanius, Bishop of Salamis, who wrote: "We fast till the ninth hour on the fourth day and the eve of the Sabbath, because the Lord was arrested at the beginning of the fourth day and crucified on the eve of the Sabbath."

There are many questions surrounding this subject. What are the implications of having diverging writings, or what is the meaning behind the phrase "rise from the dead" as well as the phrase "be in the heart of the earth three days and three nights"? These are questions that should not be answered by a book but by introspection. We will leave those questions for inquisitive minds to pursue, for there is already much to digest within this book, and our main purpose is not to start a new controversy but to settle a very old one.

The Book of Revelation then continues: "And in that hour there was a great earthquake, and the tenth of the city fell, and seven thousand names of men were slain in the earthquake" (Revelation 11:13). When using the phrase "the tenth of the city fell," the words of Isaiah are being recalled concerning the time when he said that even what was left from the previous downfall of Jerusalem was going to be destroyed again: "But a tenth part shall still be therein, and it shall return and be eaten" (Isaiah 6:13).

While concerning the seven thousand, in their efforts to look logical and correct in grammatical terms, many Bible translations have made the mistake of writing "seven thousand men were killed," but the original Greek version actually says that "seven thousand names of men were killed" in the earthquake. By saying "names of men," the author is indicating that their deaths were not physical, but a loss of honor or reputation of those people.

In Judea, there was a class of people for whom the name, that is, the genealogy or surname, was of the utmost importance since their status depended on it. We are talking about the priestly line of Judea, whose members had to prove that they were descendants of Aaron. The priestly class was composed of twenty-four clans that served in the temple on a rotating basis. Each clan had to serve for one week twice a year and had to select from among their own members a group of priests that would be responsible for carrying out those tasks in the temple.

It is estimated that from those twenty-four clans, approximately 7,200 priests were assigned to perform the services of the Temple of Jerusalem throughout the Jewish calendar. Estimations for the number of priests of that time can be found in the book *Jerusalem at the Time of Jesus*, written by Joachim Jeremias; he based his calculations on several reliable Jewish writings. From each clan, around 300 priests had to be assigned to the temple. If there were twenty-four clans, the total number of priests assigned to the temple was approximately 7,200 priests, serving in groups of 300 on a rotating basis during each year.

The honor of these ordinary priests collapsed when the High Priest Caiaphas condemned Jesus to death, who was innocent and more than righteous. The indignation could not have been small among the followers of Jesus, and, in a similar manner, many others probably also felt contempt towards the priests who plotted such injustice.

After the seven thousand "names of men" fell, the Book of Revelation goes on to say:

> *And the seventh messenger did sound, and there came great voices in the heaven, saying, 'The kingdoms of the world did become those of our Lord and of His Christ, and he shall reign to the ages of the ages!'...Thine anger did come, and the time of the dead, to be judged, and to give the reward to Thy servants, to the prophets, and to the saints, and to those fearing Thy name... And opened was the sanctuary of God in the heaven, and there was seen the ark of His covenant in His sanctuary. (Revelation 11:15-19)*

According to the letter, when the seventh angel sounds the trumpet, the kingdoms of the world become kingdoms of "our Lord and of His Christ," the reward is given to the prophets, and the temple of God is opened in heaven. All of this points to the fact that what had just happened is the pillar of the narrative. This is another indication that those words are referring precisely to the extraordinary feat accomplished by Jesus. For that reason, just before dying, in John 19:30, Jesus says, "It is finished," and in a similar manner, Mark 15:38 and Matthew 27:51 use an interesting analogy to describe the moment of his death by saying that "the veil of the temple was rent in two from the top to the bottom."

However, the story was just beginning; the great legacy of Jesus consists in opening the eyes of men from that time as well as future generations, something that the dragon, the first beast and the false prophet, also known as the second beast, would fiercely oppose.

WHEN THE THUNDERS SPEAK

With the moon under her feet

> *And a great sign was seen in the heaven, a woman arrayed with the sun, and the moon under her feet, and upon her head a crown of twelve stars, and being with child she doth cry out, travailing and pained to bring forth. And there was seen another sign in the heaven, and, lo, a great red dragon, having seven heads and ten horns, and upon his head seven diadems. (Revelation 12:1-3)*

The woman with the crown of twelve stars appears immediately after the sounding of the seventh trumpet because she represents the followers of Jesus, led by the twelve disciples. The woman is clothed with knowledge and has the moon under her feet. The moon is a symbol that represents the rituals and festivities of the Temple of Jerusalem. This derives from the fact that its religious calendar was governed by the lunar cycle, and all the sacrifices and holy days took place strictly according to the dates calculated from the first appearance of the thin crescent moon of each month.

Such was the importance of the thin crescent moon that the Jewish authorities did not start the month until they had eyewitnesses of the event occurring in the sky. Even more, whenever the phrase "beginning of the month" is mentioned in the Pentateuch, the original version in fact uses the Greek word νεομηνίαις, which means a new moon.

The moon was a symbol of all the customs and rituals of the ancient doctrine. In that sense, the words of Isaiah are strong and clear when he illustrates how the Creator despises the superficial nature of those traditions: "Hear the words of Jehovah... Your new moons and your set seasons hath My soul hated, They have been upon me for a burden, I have been weary of bearing" (Isaiah 1:14).

Saying that the woman has the moon under her feet is a way of expressing that the communities formed by Jesus' followers were above those vain rituals and festivities of the temple, whose dates,

JESUS AGAINST THE FIG TREE

as mentioned previously, were derived from the lunar cycle. The New Testament, on multiple occasions, mentions cases in which the followers of Jesus argue why they were not bound to the sacrifices of the temple, while stressing that such rites do not cleanse the sins. Nowadays, such an idea may seem obvious, but during the first century, refusing to participate in the sacrifices was a reprehensible attitude that caused numerous persecutions against the first Christians. When droughts, conflicts or other calamities occurred, the Jewish priests and Pharisees blamed the Christians for such evils by assuring that God had brought those misfortunes to the earth because Jesus' followers did not make the corresponding sacrifices. When Christians fled to the Decapolis, the Jewish leaders accused them before the pagans since the Greek culture also believed in the need to make animal sacrifices to ward off evil. For that reason, they had to endure persecutions both in Judea and in the Hellenic cities.

They knew the way to the truth, and when danger was at the door, they preferred changing their dwelling place and not their way of thinking. They did not let themselves be frightened by the executioners nor by the anxiety of life, nor did they allow themselves to be seduced by riches. In addition, they trusted more in the word of the Creator that was written in their hearts rather than the vain rites and cruel laws described in papyri.

Nevertheless, the threat was closing in. The paramount legacy and the followers of the truth were in imminent danger from the all-powerful red dragon, whose intentions would also be carried on by a beast with similar features. Great authority was given to both the red dragon and the first beast, and they used unscrupulous methods to crush their enemies; however, both of them had a different nature to that of the second beast, which is also called the false prophet whose number is the 666. But before discussing further details concerning the latter, first, it is necessary to understand the meaning of the red dragon and the first beast as well as the motive behind their insatiable thirst for blood.

The red dragon

As for the dragon with the seven heads and ten horns, later on, the letter of Revelation offers us relevant information to determine its identity along with the meaning of the woman carried by it:

> And I saw the woman drunk with the blood of the saints, and with the blood of the witnesses of Jesus. And I wondered, seeing her, with great wonder. And the angel said to me, Why hast thou wondered? I will tell thee the mystery of the woman, and of the beast which carries her, which has the seven heads and the ten horns. The beast which thou sawest was, and is not, and is about to come up out of the abyss and go into destruction: and they who dwell on the earth, whose names are not written from the founding of the world in the book of life, shall wonder, seeing the beast, that it was, and is not, and shall be present. Here is the mind that has wisdom: The seven heads are seven mountains, whereon the woman sits. And there are seven kings: five have fallen, one is, the other has not yet come; and when he comes he must remain only a little while. And the beast that was and is not, he also is an eighth, and is of the seven, and goes into destruction. And the ten horns which thou sawest are ten kings, which have not yet received a kingdom, but receive authority as kings one hour with the beast. (Revelation 17:6-12)

The woman drunk with the blood of the prophets is Jerusalem; even Jesus referred to such a city as the place where prophets were murdered time after time.

Concerning the seven heads, five of which had already fallen, one was reigning, and another was still to come, the author is giving us another reference point in time since during the years of Jesus' ministry, the Kingdom of Judah had been governed by five foreign powers that had already fallen: Babylon, Persia, Greece, the Ptolemaic Empire of Egypt and the Seleucid Empire of Syria. It was now being governed to some extent by the Roman Empire, the sixth head, which later—during the First Jewish-Roman War—would be replaced by a radical Jewish government, the seventh head of the beast, that would not last for too long. The book is referring to this particular event when it says, "the other has not yet come; and when he comes he must remain only a little while" (Revelation 17:10). The rebel government was established during the last months of 66 CE, and it lasted just a few years.

The radical Jewish rebels only reigned for about 42 months, that is three years and a half, but their actions unleashed a series of catastrophic events that brought great suffering to the Jewish people and ended in the second destruction of Jerusalem by the middle of 70 CE, on this occasion by the hand of the Roman forces. They annihilated the rebels, expelled most Jews from Jerusalem and reestablished Roman control over the province of Judea, this time with full authority. "...and the beast that was, and is not, he also is eighth, and out of the seven he is, and to destruction he doth go away" (Revelation 17:11).

The ten horns represent the Decapolis, a Greek term meaning ten cities, which was commonly used when referring to a group of Hellenic cities that were also located in the land of Canaan, most of them on the eastern side of the Jordan River. They were relevant not only because they were taken into consideration by Jesus when he was spreading his words and are mentioned throughout the New Testament, but also because they played a key historical role during the first century. These ten cities were inhabited by both people with Greek customs and Jews, and both cultures coexisted peacefully most of the time. Still, the Jewish revolt brought violent conflicts between those two peoples. One of those ten cities, Pella in the region of Perea, even became the place where Jewish Christians emigrated when fleeing from the Jewish revolt and the persecutions that other Jews were carrying out against them.

> *And the dragon stood before the woman who was about to bring forth, in order that when she brought forth he might devour her child. And she brought forth a male son, who shall shepherd all the nations with an iron rod; and her child was caught up to God and to his throne. And the woman fled into the wilderness, where she has there a place prepared of God, that they should nourish her there a thousand two hundred and sixty days. And there was war in the heaven: Michael and his angels went to war with the dragon... And the great dragon was cast out, the ancient serpent, he who is called Devil and Satan... And when the dragon saw that he had been cast out into the earth, he persecuted the woman which bore the male child. And there were given to the woman the two wings of the great eagle, that she might fly into the desert into her place, where she is nourished there a time, and times, and half a time, from the face of the serpent. And the serpent cast out of his mouth behind the woman water as a river, that he might make her be as one carried away by a river. (Revelation 12:4-15)*

The battle between the dragon and Michael represents the doctrinal and spiritual debate that emerged during the first century between Jesus' teachings and the religion of the temple's priests. The moment the dragon is cast out from heaven is the time when the priests' doctrine ceased to be considered the unquestionable truth by many Jewish people who ultimately decided to follow the teachings of Jesus, an event that enraged the dragon, which then started persecuting Christians throughout the earth. When it is said that the women clothed with the sun fled away from the dragon to the wilderness in order to be nourished for 1,260 days, the author is referring to the time when the Jewish Christians emigrated to the Decapolis, to Pella in particular, escaping persecutions and other conflicts that peaked during the Jewish rebel government that lasted three years and a half. Such immigration of Christians is mentioned by Eusebius, one of the first Christian historians of the third century.

A beast with authority for 42 months

> *And I saw a beast rising out of the sea, having ten horns and seven heads, and upon its horns ten diadems, and upon its heads names of blasphemy. And the beast which I saw was like to a leopardess, and its feet as of a bear, and its mouth as a lion's mouth; and the dragon gave to it his power, and his throne, and great authority; and one of his heads was as slain to death, and his wound of death had been healed: and the whole earth wondered after the beast. And they did homage to the dragon, because he gave the authority to the beast; and they did homage to the beast, saying, Who is like to the beast? and who can make war with it? And there was given to it a mouth, speaking great things and blasphemies; and there was given to it authority to pursue its career forty-two months. (Revelation 13:1-5)*

As mentioned earlier, forty-two months—three years and a half—is the lifespan of the government that was established by the Jewish rebels throughout Judea and Galilee after expelling the Romans from the region in 66 CE.

This beast that was rising out of the sea also had seven heads and ten horns, just as the red dragon before it. This is so because the concept behind both the first beast and the red dragon is the same, with only slight differences that come from the sequence of events, which are: a different ruling head and the fact that this beast had crowns on its horns. When the red dragon appeared in the previous chapter of Revelation, it was still under the authority of its sixth head, as it is explained later in chapter 17 of the same book with the phrase: "there are seven kings: five have fallen, one is, the other has not yet come; and when he comes he must remain only a little while." While the beast that emerged right after the red dragon was already under the authority of the seventh head, which can be assumed from the fact that authority was given to it only for forty-two months, just as it was said that the seventh head would "remain only a little while." Its duration was short, but it had enormous consequences for the Jewish people because, in addition to the many lives that were lost throughout Judea due to the rebellion, it also meant the definitive destruction of the temple and the last time that Jerusalem was in the hands of Jewish authorities.

This particular beast had crowns on its ten horns because the Decapolis, which opposed the Jewish rebel government, had the full support of the Roman Empire to counteract the Jewish revolt, that is, a foreign power gave a certain level of authority to the group of ten cities.

The images of a bear, a leopard and a lion are taken from the words written in chapter 7 of the Book of Daniel, where the Jewish prophet describes the main empires of his time with such symbolism. There is already broad consensus that the three kingdoms to which Daniel was referring were Babylon, represented by the lion with wings; Persia, represented by the bear with the three ribs in the mouth; and Greece is the four-headed leopard. The logic behind such an interpretation of that particular section of the Book of Daniel is straightforward and already known by most; thus, we will not get into further explanation of Daniel's words, but we will focus on the fact that the author of Revelation uses his same words when describing the beast that was given authority for 42 months. This is so because the culture and identity of the Jewish people had been greatly influenced by those three empires since the time they were ruled by them and, as such, the recently established Jewish Kingdom seemed as if it had been born from those foreign powers of antiquity.

When the Jewish rebels managed to annihilate the Roman garrison in Jerusalem in the year 66 CE, and then they were able to defeat the Romans in the first battles and drive them out of the province, such a feat caused great astonishment, as it was unimaginable to think that the troops of the mighty Roman Empire could be defeated. But while many radical Jews were in awe of the new government they had established by force, the Christians and Jewish Christians saw it differently and emigrated to Pella of Perea, in the Decapolis. In accordance with the warning that Jesus had given them many years before, the Christians moved to Pella due to the fact that more armed conflicts between the Jewish rebels and the Romans were coming, and the followers of Jesus opposed all kinds of violence; but what is even worse, being under a completely autonomous and radical Jewish government could mean an intensification of the persecutions against Christians. If in previous years the Jewish priests persecuted them even though the region was still under the control of the Roman Empire, they would do so yet with more severity under an independent government headed by the high priest of the Temple of Jerusalem, whose laws and doctrines, in addition to being in clear opposition to the teachings of Jesus, ordered to kill those Jews who accepted such teachings.

"And I saw one of his heads as the wound of death, and the wound of his death was healed: and all the earth wondered after the beast" (Revelation 13:3). No one would ever imagine it, not even the Jews themselves, that after their last kingdom had ceased to exist, they would be able to reestablish a Jewish government throughout the region of Judea and Galilee, but this was in fact the case; the head with the deadly wound was healed and given the power to act for 42 months and to overcome the saints. However, the remaining Jewish Christian community fled and hid for 1,260 days, that is, 42 months.

Despite all their power, neither the dragon nor the beast that rose from the sea would cause as much damage to the legacy of Jesus and his followers as did the second beast—the false prophet—, whose power was not limited only to the destruction of the body, but it also had the ability to seize the soul of men through persuasion, and it continues to do so even to this day.

9

THE FALSE PROPHET

The mystery of the false prophet

Although his words may mimic the light, a deceiver cannot prevent the consequences of his actions from being obscure. If a man works miracles assuring that they are being done in the name of God, but his instructions resemble evil acts, what will you believe in, in his miracles or in his teachings? "Verily, verily, I say to you, He that enters not in by the door to the fold of the sheep, but mounts up elsewhere, he is a thief and a robber...The thief comes not but that he may steal, and kill, and destroy" (John 10:1-10).

The identity of the false prophet is one of the most obscure mysteries of the Book of Revelation and has become one of the best kept secrets in the history of theology and Christianity. As a result, dozens of different interpretations have come out concerning the mystery of the second beast, which rises from the earth having two horns like a lamb but speaking like a dragon. The many different interpretations range from a historical perspective to the most sensationalist explanations. Some theologians state that this figure was a Roman emperor, while many others affirm that he is someone that would emerge in the future. But, despite their good intentions, both sides are still far from the truth.

Those who assume that he was a Roman emperor resort to all sorts of mathematical equations, which are unknown by the majority, to arrive at an elegant but erroneous conclusion; while those who believe in the theory that he is a figure from the future always end up assuming that the false prophet would appear at a particular moment during their own lifetimes. The latter also believe that this event would bring along the end of the world as we know it. However, the beast whose number is 666 cannot be confined to a particular point in time because its influence has already reached unimaginable limits; its power has transcended time and cultures. The beast was present long before the Book of Revelation, it was there while John was writing the letter, and it is still here among us.

It is not complicated to decipher the meaning of the number 666 and you do not have to be an expert in codes or a historian. It is much simpler than that. The identity of the beast can be revealed without having to look further than the Bible itself. Neither complex calculations nor exaggerated assumptions are required; counting his name will suffice.

Counting the number of the beast

The identity of the beast can be found in the Bible itself, whose words offer a clear and definitive proof that exposes the false prophet.

> *Here is wisdom. He that has understanding let him count the number of the beast: for it is a man's number; and its number is six hundred and sixty-six. (Revelation 13:18)*

The previous paragraph contains one of the most relevant phrases of the entire letter of Revelation. It holds an essential key to unmask the identity of the false prophet, which in turn leads to the

THE FALSE PROPHET

understanding of the true message of the writing. When it is said, "count the number of the beast ... six hundred and sixty-six", the writing gives us the most powerful clue, yet the most threatening one to the author's life because if his true intentions were uncovered, he would inevitably be stoned to death.

To determine what or who is the beast that speaks like a dragon and deceives men by working miracles, it is necessary to do only what the author of the letter tells us: count. But count what? Count where? The author of the Book of Revelation would not encode a message that was impossible to decipher; he just had to use concepts that were easy to understand by the unbiased mind but were confusing for the prejudiced ones. In this manner, only those who were spiritually mature would be able to understand a message that could mean death for him who wrote it and, at the same time, was full of life and hope for those who would receive it.

Within the books of the Bible, there is a figure whose name in Greek is repeated six hundred and sixty-six times until the moment of his death. That figure has shaped our minds, our religions and even our laws. Over the course of millennia, he has been turning hearts to stone to the point where man becomes incapable of understanding the message of Jesus in all its splendor. That has been the most devastating harm the false prophet has inflicted on man; for the teachings of Jesus are meant to be followed to their full extent, but the beast instructs men to stop halfway along the path or even destroys the path entirely.

The identity of the false prophet is certainly within the words of the Bible. But in order to identify him, one must first find a version of the Bible that resembles as much as possible the original text that the followers of Jesus used during the first century. Today, there are hundreds of different versions of the Bible, and the creation of each one involved a process in which the translator or scribe was required to add or delete certain words so that the meaning is naturally coherent and fluent in their respective languages. For this reason, it is vital to have access to the original Greek text since what we are looking for is hidden within its lines.

The most reliable Greek Pentateuch

Although the Book of Revelation belongs to the New Testament, the key to discovering the identity of the false prophet and the meaning of the 666 lies within the words of the Pentateuch. Thus, it is essential to first identify the version of the Old Testament that was most often used among the early followers of Jesus. We are referring to the Septuagint, the well-known Greek translation of the Old Testament whose origins date back to the third and second century BC. The Septuagint was made in a time when Koine Greek was becoming the dominant language in the region, and for hundreds of years it became one of the most used versions of the Old Testament, including in the first century. There is a broad consensus that the Septuagint was the version of the Old Testament the apostles quoted in most cases.

Knowing that followers of Jesus had access to the Greek Septuagint leads us in the right direction, but this fact is not enough when today there are different versions of that particular translation circulating. Hence, we must also determine which of those versions is the most reliable at the present time. Thanks to the field of study known as textual criticism, there is one edition of the Septuagint that is a very accurate reconstruction of the original Greek text. These types of editions are called critical texts because they seek to resemble the original text, word by word, as much as possible.

The process by which textual criticism reconstructs ancient manuscripts is not an easy task; significant resources and valuable time have to be spent to establish a critical text. To achieve this goal, people specializing in textual criticism create a complete text by carefully analyzing the reliability of all the existing manuscripts and

THE FALSE PROPHET

fragments, depending on their age, reputation, source and affinity with one another.

As a result of that hard work, in 1935 the biblical scholar Alfred Rahlfs, with the help of others, published a highly accurate edition of the Septuagint with a version of the Pentateuch that is rigorous enough for our purposes. Since its publication, the Rahlfs' Septuagint has been considered one of the most reliable sources for in-depth studies of the Bible.

Considering that the Rahlfs' edition of the Septuagint contains a word-by-word reconstruction of the Pentateuch, we may now proceed and be confident that this is the appropriate version of the Old Testament to unveil the meaning of the number 666 and reveal the identity of the beast.

Exposing the identity of the false prophet

To unmask the false prophet in categorical manner, we have to count his name. The letter of Revelation gives us enough clues to know where to look. The second beast is a false prophet who deceives men by means of the miraculous signs he is allowed to do in the presence of the first beast. Even Jesus' words and deeds give us guidance about who or what could represent the second beast, considering that the conduct of the false prophet outright opposes the pillars of Jesus' teachings. "And it works great signs, that it should cause even fire to come down from heaven to the earth before men. And it deceives those that dwell upon the earth by reason of the signs which it was given to it to work before the beast" (Revelation 13:13-14).

Although the characteristics that are described concerning the second beast already give us a clear idea concerning the identity of the false prophet, only after proving that he also meets the last and most peculiar condition—that in which counting the number of his name yields 666—could we confirm categorically who this figure is.

WHEN THE THUNDERS SPEAK

In the most reliable version of the Greek Pentateuch, there is a biblical figure whose name is repeated exactly 666 times throughout his life. That name is Moses.

Starting from the first time his name is written in Exodus 2:10 until the moment of his death in Deuteronomy 34:5, the name of Moses is mentioned 666 times. "Here is wisdom. He that has understanding let him count the number of the beast: for it is a man's number; and its number is six hundred and sixty-six."

The count begins when the Pharaoh's daughter gives him a name: "And when the child was grown, she brought him to Pharaoh's daughter, and he became her son. And she called his name Moses" (Exodus 2:10). And once we get to the verse that narrates his death, right at that instance, the name of Moses has already been mentioned 666 times. "And Moses the servant of Jehovah died there" (Deuteronomy 34:5). With that verse, the counting of his name is finished and the meaning of the number 666 is revealed, unmasking the identity of the false prophet in a conclusive manner.

The counting must be done in the Rahlfs' edition of the Septuagint, which contains the most accurate text of the original Greek translation of the Pentateuch. In the Rahlfs' Septuagint, the name of Moses in Greek is written as Μωϋσῆς, but it can have different endings depending on its function in a sentence. Throughout the Pentateuch, his name appears in the following ways: Μωϋσῆς, Μωυσῆν, Μωυσῆ, Μωυσῇ and Μωυσεῖ.

All of these noun cases of the name of Moses must be taken into account: Μωϋσῆς corresponds to the nominative case, which is used when the name is the subject in a sentence; Μωυσῆν for the accusative case, which is used as a direct object; Μωυσῆ for vocative or genitive cases; and Μωυσῇ and Μωυσεῖ for the dative case, used mostly when the name is an indirect object. Table 1 and 2 show the number of times the name of Moses is mentioned until Deuteronomy 34:5, which is the moment of his death.

THE FALSE PROPHET

Table 1. Instances of the name per chapter until the moment of his death in Deuteronomy 34:5

EXODUS		LEVITICUS		NUMBERS		DEUTERONOMY	
Ch. 1	0	Ch. 1	1	Ch. 1	6	Ch. 1	3
Ch. 2	9	Ch. 2	0	Ch. 2	3	Ch. 2	0
Ch. 3	11	Ch. 3	0	Ch. 3	14	Ch. 3	0
Ch. 4	17	Ch. 4	1	Ch. 4	13	Ch. 4	4
Ch. 5	4	Ch. 5	2	Ch. 5	4	Ch. 5	1
Ch. 6	13	Ch. 6	3	Ch. 6	2	Ch. 6	0
Ch. 7	9	Ch. 7	3	Ch. 7	5	Ch. 7	0
Ch. 8	13	Ch. 8	33	Ch. 8	8	Ch. 8	0
Ch. 9	12	Ch. 9	9	Ch. 9	7	Ch. 9	0
Ch. 10	14	Ch. 10	12	Ch. 10	5	Ch. 10	0
Ch. 11	6	Ch. 11	1	Ch. 11	14	Ch. 11	0
Ch. 12	7	Ch. 12	1	Ch. 12	10	Ch. 12	0
Ch. 13	3	Ch. 13	1	Ch. 13	7	Ch. 13	0
Ch. 14	8	Ch. 14	2	Ch. 14	10	Ch. 14	0
Ch. 15	4	Ch. 15	1	Ch. 15	8	Ch. 15	0
Ch. 16	18	Ch. 16	3	Ch. 16	12	Ch. 16	0
Ch. 17	14	Ch. 17	1	Ch. 17	18	Ch. 17	0
Ch. 18	18	Ch. 18	1	Ch. 18	1	Ch. 18	0
Ch. 19	14	Ch. 19	1	Ch. 19	1	Ch. 19	0
Ch. 20	4	Ch. 20	1	Ch. 20	12	Ch. 20	0
Ch. 21	0	Ch. 21	3	Ch. 21	9	Ch. 21	0
Ch. 22	0	Ch. 22	3	Ch. 22	0	Ch. 22	0
Ch. 23	0	Ch. 23	6	Ch. 23	0	Ch. 23	0
Ch. 24	13	Ch. 24	5	Ch. 24	0	Ch. 24	0
Ch. 25	1	Ch. 25	1	Ch. 25	5	Ch. 25	0
Ch. 26	0	Ch. 26	1	Ch. 26	8	Ch. 26	0
Ch. 27	0	Ch. 27	2	Ch. 27	9	Ch. 27	3
Ch. 28	0			Ch. 28	1	Ch. 28	1
Ch. 29	0			Ch. 29	0	Ch. 29	1
Ch. 30	4			Ch. 30	4	Ch. 30	0
Ch. 31	3			Ch. 31	21	Ch. 31	11
Ch. 32	17			Ch. 32	8	Ch. 32	4
Ch. 33	9			Ch. 33	3	Ch. 33	2
Ch. 34	16			Ch. 34	4	Ch. 34:1-5	3
Ch. 35	5			Ch. 35	2	Until the moment of his death in Deuteronomy 34:5	
Ch. 36	11			Ch. 36	4		
Ch. 37	2						
Ch. 38	2						
Ch. 39	6						
Ch. 40	10						
297		**98**		**238**		**33**	

297 + 98 + 238 + 33 = 666

Note: the counting must be done in the Rahlfs' Septuagint, which contains the most accurate version of the Greek Pentateuch. Text and location of various verses differ from modern translations.

Table 2. Instances of the name for each Greek noun case until the moment of his death in Deuteronomy 34:5

GREEK NOUN CASE	EXODUS	LEVITICUS	NUMBERS	DEUTERONOMY Until his death in Deut. 34:5	TOTAL PER GREEK NOUN CASE
Μωϋσῆς	153	42	95	28	**318**
Μωυσῆν	88	38	88	4	**218**
Μωυσῆ	20	3	24	0	**47**
Μωυσῆ	30	15	31	1	**77**
Μωυσεῖ	6	0	0	0	**6**
			TOTAL		**666**

The fact that his name is mentioned exactly 666 times until the moment of his death, and that it happens to occur in the most reliable version of the Greek Pentateuch, is a clear indication and not a coincidence. In addition to this, the other descriptions concerning the false prophet also fit in every way the profile of this prominent and immensely influential figure.

After knowing the true meaning of the number 666, it becomes much easier to understand the other clues of the riddle, especially those related to the description of the false prophet. The first words used to describe him are as follows: "And I saw another beast rising out of the earth; and it had two horns like to a lamb, and spoke as a dragon" (Revelation 13:11). To understand this phrase, one must remember that the lamb is a symbol of meekness, as expressed in Isaiah 53:7 and Jeremiah 11:19; thus, the Book of Revelation implies that the false prophet appears to be meek, but in fact he speaks like

THE FALSE PROPHET

a dragon. The author resorts to this analogy because the Pentateuch claims that Moses was a very meek man, even though his actions indicated otherwise. For example, the book of Numbers 12:3 says: "But the man Moses was very meek, above all men that were upon the face of the earth." Nevertheless, that Moses was the same one who did not hesitate to condemn to death anyone who did not follow his laws. He unleashed a sea of destruction upon any person for the slightest fault, alleging that his cruel decrees were instructions dictated by God. The cases already cited concerning Numbers 15:32-26 and Leviticus 24:11-16 speak for themselves.

Another example is the occasion when Moses was angry with the captains of his army because they captured alive the women and the male children of the Midianites. He reproached the captains and told them: "And now slay every male among the little ones, and slay every woman that hath known man by lying with him" (Numbers 31:17). We can also recall the episode in which he ordered men to kill their own brothers or neighbors who had participated in idolatry: "And he said to them, Thus saith Jehovah, the God of Israel: Put every man his sword upon his hip; go and return from gate to gate through the camp, and slay every man his brother, and every man his friend, and every man his neighbour. And the sons of Levi did according to the word of Moses; and there fell of the people that day about three thousand men" (Exodus 32:27-28).

Tributes to arrogance and oppression do not end there. Within the books of the Pentateuch, which were supposedly written by Moses, there are many other cases in which he dictates decrees so oppressive that it would seem as if he were speaking like a dragon. If the person we are referring to was the meekest man on earth, as stated in Numbers 12:3, then humankind has yet to know one perverse and tyrant man.

Another clue from the Book of Revelation that becomes evident after having understood the meaning of the number 666 is the one that refers to the great signs that the false prophet is able to do with fire: "And it works great signs, that it should cause even fire to come down from heaven to the earth before men" (Revelation 13:13).

Indeed, that false prophet is recognized as the man who supposedly performed the most sensational miracles with fire, which he used as a sign of power or fury. "And the whole of mount Sinai smoked, because Jehovah descended on it in fire; and its smoke ascended as the smoke of a furnace; and the whole mountain shook greatly" (Exodus 19:18). He also performed great signs with fire in Exodus 9:23, where allegedly "Moses stretched out his staff toward the heavens, and Jehovah gave thunder and hail; and the fire ran along the ground." And he used fire in a miraculous way to burn the sacrifices: "And Moses and Aaron went into the tent of meeting, and came out and blessed the people; and the glory of Jehovah appeared to all the people. And there went out fire from before Jehovah, and consumed on the altar the burnt-offering, and the pieces of fat; and all the people saw it, and they shouted, and fell on their face" (Leviticus 9:23-24).

The false prophet also used the power of fire to destroy men: "And there went out fire from before Jehovah, and devoured them, and they died before Jehovah. And Moses said to Aaron, this is what Jehovah spoke, saying, I will be hallowed in them that come near me..." (Leviticus 10:2-3). While the book of Numbers says: "And there came out a fire from Jehovah, and consumed the two hundred and fifty men that had presented incense. And Jehovah spoke to Moses, saying, Speak to Eleazar the son of Aaron the priest, that he take up the censers out of the burning; and scatter the fire afar; for they are hallowed" (Numbers 16:35-37).

According to the ancient writings, there was no other man who performed as many miracles as the Moses of the Pentateuch. This leads us to the following statement concerning the false prophet: "And it deceives those that dwell upon the earth by reason of the

THE FALSE PROPHET

signs which it was given to it to work before the beast" (Revelation 13:14).

Note that the Book of Revelation also refers to the false prophet as the second beast, which works great signs in the presence of the first one. The great fame of the Moses of the Pentateuch arises from the assumption that he was the only prophet who performed great signs in front of an entire nation—that is, in the presence of the first beast—. In that way, he deceives people because the eyes of men worship vain demonstrations of power more than humbleness and mercy. However, a true messenger of the Creator is not a man who works miracles to justify his obscure deeds, but a man that with his goods deeds makes evident his miracles.

> *And it was given to it to give breath to the image of the beast, that the image of the beast should also speak, and should cause that as many as should not do homage to the image of the beast should be killed. (Revelation 13:15)*

With these words the author refers to the Laws of the Pentateuch since, besides being a perennial image of the beast, it was as if the ancient writings were alive. For they had the power to decide who should die according to its cruel commandments, and both the priests and most of the people followed its decrees without delay.

In the same chapter, the letter of Revelation also says:

> *And it causes all, the small and the great, and the rich and the poor, and the free and the bondmen, that they should give them a mark upon their right hand or upon their forehead; and that no one should be able to buy or sell save he that had the mark, the name of the beast, or the number of its name. (Revelation 13:16-17)*

These mysterious words also become clear when reading carefully the Pentateuch, for on three occasions those writings mention an identical concept. Exodus 13:16, as well as Deuteronomy 6:8 and 11:18, use similar words concerning the adherence to the laws contained in them: "And thou shalt bind them for a sign on thy hand, and they shall be for frontlets between thine eyes" (Deuteronomy 6:8). Even though many people from antiquity took these verses literally and started wearing phylacteries in their arms and foreheads, which also gave rise to a debate on whether it should be worn on the left or right arm, the truth of the matter is that this phrase from Deuteronomy was figurative language to stress how the law of the Pentateuch should be in their minds and actions, and the right hand has always been used to symbolize ones' actions.

The statement that nobody could sell or buy, except those who had the mark, comes from the circumstances of that time. The letter of Revelation is talking about a time when there was a great polarization fueled by the radical Jewish government that was established in 66 CE., whose measures in relation to the temple service became increasingly strict against foreigners. The radical government was controlled first by the Pharisees and Sadducees and later by the Zealots and Sicarii. These groups called themselves Jews, but they were not who they claimed to be; for true Jews are not bound by the violent laws of the Pentateuch but by the wisdom of Isaiah.

As the Jewish government became more radicalized, it adopted an aggressive attitude not only towards non-Jews but also against the more conciliatory Jews. The polarization grew even deeper with the constant battles that the government of the insurrection waged against the Roman army and the Gentiles throughout the region of Canaan. Because of this dire situation, it is just logical to assume that the radical government implemented the same strict policies that were adopted in the region around the year 300 BC when the Gentiles were not allowed to be near the temple. This meant that foreigners could not participate in the transactions that were

THE FALSE PROPHET

regularly carried out for the offerings and sacrifices, and that a similar situation would be generated under the new government. Writings from the first century talk about the state of affairs before and during the emergence of the new radical government:

> *Eleazar, the son of Ananias the high priest, a very bold youth, who was at that time governor of the temple, persuaded those that officiated in the Divine service to receive no gift or sacrifice for any foreigner. And this was the true beginning of our war with the Romans; for they rejected the sacrifice of Caesar on this account. (The Wars of the Jews, book 2, chapter 17, paragraph 2)*

It is also important to remember that many Jews considered the Gentiles to be impure, especially in matters related to the Temple of Jerusalem. Consequently, the new government of the year 66 CE, comprised to a large extent of the most radical factions of Judaism, had strong motives to prohibit, either officially or informally, the participation of the Gentiles in the purchase or sale of grain flour, animals and other items that practitioners presented as offerings at the altar. These transactions were reserved for those who had the mark that was mentioned earlier.

After presenting all those descriptions concerning the false prophet, the author of the Book of Revelation then proceeds to give us the definitive clue that would clear up any doubt on this matter: "Here is wisdom. He that has understanding let him count the number of the beast: for it is a man's number; and its number is six hundred and sixty-six" (Revelation 13:18).

The letter of Revelation becomes an open book after understanding the enigmatic 666, whose meaning we have already explained. All the illustrations and each one of the mysterious words of the Book of Revelation were written in that manner for a very particular reason. The intention was clear; it was neither to create sensationalism nor to make its content incomprehensible. It was written in such a way that it would be able to survive the permanent threat that it had to face and, at some point, enlighten those men and women who would be able to understand the words within the writing.

All the aforementioned elements are sufficient to decipher the identity of the false prophet, the second beast, whose cruel norms, vain rituals and mundane attitudes have been hardening the heart of man for millennia. The Pentateuch was being used to adulterate and destroy the teachings of both Jesus and the true Jewish prophets.

Nevertheless, there is still another important question that must be addressed concerning the false prophet of the Pentateuch. Why does the Book of Revelation, in a later chapter, make reference to the name of Moses in a positive light? The writing mentions the name of Moses explicitly just once, and it does so at the moment of victory over the beast, its image and its number.

In antiquity there were people, both Jews and Christians, who knew that the Moses of the Pentateuch was a distorted and perverted representation of the real Moses. They affirmed that the real Moses was a righteous man, a servant of God, whose name could be cleared only when the false stories and doctrines of the Law were unmasked and thrown away at last. So many persecutions have occurred and so many scrolls have been burned that the only information left about those people who had such hopes is found in the writings of those who considered them as enemies and heretics.

Some of them are mentioned in the *Panarion* of Epiphanius of Salamis, whose opinion appear to be biased in some instances, but he is one of the few sources left where we can find some information regarding the subject. In the first book of the *Panarion*, while speaking against a Jewish-Christian religious group from the first century known as the Ebionites, Epiphanius says that such a group does not accept the Pentateuch in its entirety and that they would blaspheme most of the Law. And while he was speaking against a

THE FALSE PROPHET

Jewish denomination called Nasaraeans—not to be confused neither with Nazoreans nor Nazarites—, Epiphanius states that they believed in Moses but not in the one from the Pentateuch, which according to them was a forgery that contained customs that were not instituted by the patriarchs.

We are not stating that the Book Revelation was written by one of those groups. Rather, our purpose here is to illustrate that in the first century, and even before that time, it was not uncommon to hold the belief that the real Moses was not the same man described in the Pentateuch. The letter of Revelation is a magnificent writing that not only restores the teachings of Jesus, but it also clears the name of the real Moses while condemning the one from the Pentateuch. This is illustrated by the following verses:

> *And I saw as a glass sea, mingled with fire, and those that had gained the victory over the beast, and over its image, and over the number of its name, standing upon the glass sea, having harps of God. And they sing the song of Moses bondman of God, and the song of the Lamb, saying, Great and wonderful are thy works, Lord God Almighty; righteous and true are thy ways, O King of Nations. (Revelation 15:2-3)*

The Moses of the true Jews was never the nefarious Moses of the Pentateuch, which was a wicked creation that added cruel instructions, idolatrous rituals, and hundreds of superficial customs and laws. All this just to manipulate the people generation after generation and to justify the evil means of the oppressors. Metaphorical poems and songs about Moses were taken literally to create outrageous stories. Simple and just instructions were stretched and twisted to a great degree by the machinations of man to mingle righteousness with wickedness, but Jesus did not accept that. He was determined to unmask the false Moses, the second beast, whose laws were also used to justify the persecutions of the early Christians, many of whom lost their lives when charges of blasphemy were brought against them by the accuser.

The accuser of our brothers

The dispute between the instructions of the false prophet and the teachings of Jesus went much further than simple doctrinal disagreements. They opposed each other in the fundamental values of man. This was a dangerous situation for both the soul and the body since the law of Moses from the Pentateuch, even centuries after it was written, was still practically alive—as if it had breath in it—because it had the power to order the killing of anyone who contradicted it. This used to happen without fail or delay when the priests did exactly as the law commanded. By using such a tool, they were able to kill Jesus after accusing him of blasphemy, and with that same law they justified the persecutions against his followers. "And it was given to it to give breath to the image of the beast, that the image of the beast should also speak, and should cause that as many as should not do homage to the image of the beast should be killed" (Revelation 13:15).

The law was clear, it ordered to kill all the people who blasphemed, that included anyone whose thinking contradicted the old doctrine.

The letter of Revelation speaks of an accuser being thrown out at the moment when the dragon that persecuted the woman is defeated:

> And I heard a great voice in the heaven saying, Now is come the salvation and the power and the kingdom of our God, and the authority of his Christ; for the accuser of our brethren has been cast out, who accused them before our God day and night. (Revelation 12:10)

THE FALSE PROPHET

Within the gospels we can find an interesting expression regarding an accuser. Although in one occasion it is written that Jesus said "for if ye had believed Moses, ye would have believed me", just before those words, he also stated the following: "Think not that I will accuse you to the Father: there is one who accuses you, Moses, on whom ye trust" (John 5:45).

But the peculiar trait of being an "accuser" takes even more shape when we bring to mind the first persecutions the priests carried out against Jesus' followers. Many of the early followers of Jesus, despite their attempts to defend themselves by alleging that they believed in Moses and in the Law, ended up being accused by the religious leaders who used precisely the name of Moses and his laws as a justification to condemn them to death. They did it by either using false witnesses or just because Jesus' followers often refused to comply with the cruel and vain commandments mandated in the ancient writings of the priests.

Vivid examples can be found in Acts 6:11, when in order to condemn Stephen, some people are bribed to make them say that they "have heard him speaking blasphemous words against Moses and God"; and Acts 18:13, where Paul is accused of persuading men "to worship God contrary to the law." Such a charge was difficult to refute considering that Paul rightly stated that "Circumcision is nothing, and uncircumcision is nothing; but keeping God's commandments" (1 Corinthians 7:19), contradicting in this way Leviticus 12:1-3, which claimed that circumcision had been established by a direct order from God: "And Jehovah spoke to Moses, saying, Speak unto the children of Israel, saying, If a woman conceive seed, and bear a male...on the eighth day shall the flesh of his foreskin be circumcised." Likewise, the book of Genesis—which according to the Jewish priests was also written by Moses—emphasizes even more the alleged importance of that trivial matter: "And the uncircumcised male who hath not been circumcised in the flesh of his foreskin, that soul shall be cut off from his peoples: he hath broken my covenant" (Genesis 17:14). Diverging views on simple matters, like the one we just mentioned, were enough to scandalize the priests to the point of brutality.

If the law of the Pentateuch had been right from the beginning instead of being tyrannical declaring death for the slightest offense, the disciples of Jesus would never have been questioned in unfair trials for displaying behaviors that were seven times more righteous than those of their accusers; and even so they were condemned. How many innocent lives would have been saved! The ignorance of man knows no limits, and very often the truth can only be conceived after centuries of reflection.

The teachings of truth have been watered-down, the accuser managed to do it over and over again. With alleged miracles and arrogant statements, he deceived those who followed him blindly, and the rest were forced to bow down with cruel methods. A teaching that was pure in nature ended up full of stains. By restraining righteousness and denying mercy, the accuser managed to defile the most consequential legacy that had been given to men.

Still, the author of the Book of Revelation did a splendid job to rescue such a legacy and cleanse it of the machinations of men. Although the accuser is prone to war, man's duty is to avoid them; although the accuser takes pride in arrogance, man must be strong and remain in meekness; although the accuser orders to kill those who break his laws; man is bound to value his neighbor's life as his own; although the accuser professes to be speaking in the name of God, it is man's job to unmask him and clear the name of the Creator for the sake of humanity.

Two paths leading in opposite directions

Certainly, the Moses of the Pentateuch is the false prophet, the beast whose name is repeated 666 times since its first occurrence in the

THE FALSE PROPHET

book of Exodus until the moment of his death. His doctrine has always been the main obstacle against the true teachings of Jesus, who brought forth irreconcilable differences in relation to the cruel laws and vain traditions of the Pentateuch.

Many will try to cling to the ancient traditions and will argue that the Pentateuch was inspired by God. This is so because the worldly perspective of man paints those stories in a way that makes them seem like glorious events that elevate the pride to inconceivable heights. But in reality, such pride seats on a very fragile throne. Within these stories, there are great and miraculous demonstrations of power that became deeply embedded in our culture, and for many of us they have become part of our lives since our childhood, but such stories are nothing more than an altar that was built to honor vanity.

To justify their devotion to those traditions, most people rely on the writing that says Jesus had not come to abolish the law, as it is indicated in Matthew 5:17; however, all his actions proved otherwise. First, Jesus openly opposed the death penalty, as was the case of forgiveness to the adulterous woman referred to by Papias—bishop of Hierapolis—in the second century, which was restated more than two centuries later by Didymus of Alexandria and then by Augustine of Hippo. The latter even reproached the constant attempts that were made to eliminate that section in the ancient writings: "Some people of little faith, or enemies of the true faith, I believe, afraid of granting impunity to their wives, removed in their manuscripts the act of forgiveness toward the adulteress" (*Augustinus, De adulterinis conjugiis*). In addition to this motive, it is logical to point out one more, a very obvious one: that of eliminating existing contradictions between Jesus and the laws of the Pentateuch.

WHEN THE THUNDERS SPEAK

According to the law of the Pentateuch, both adultery and violations of the Sabbath were worthy of execution by stoning, but Jesus was clearly against those cruel and futile decrees.

Jesus also opposed the concept of an eye for an eye that was stipulated in Exodus 21:24 and Deuteronomy 19:21: "And thine eye shall not spare: life for life, eye for eye, tooth for tooth, hand for hand..." On the other hand, Jesus always emphasized the enormous importance of forgiveness and mercy, which were values that he considered to be non-negotiable. With the intention of demonstrating that no limits should be placed on forgiveness, when Peter asked him how many times should he forgive someone, Jesus replied, "I say not to thee until seven times, but until seventy times seven." He also opposed all kinds of superficial rites, and in Mark 12:33-34 he showed how pointless the animal sacrifices were, even though such traditions had a major role in the law of the Pentateuch and some were even obligatory according to those writings.

Likewise, although the ancient law was extremely strict regarding blasphemy, which was punished with death, Jesus said in Matthew 12:31-32 that all blasphemy, even against him, will be forgiven, except when it is done against the Holy Spirit; and from his words in Luke 12:10-12, it can be inferred that by saying "blasphemy against the Holy Spirit" he is referring to the act of speaking against the voice that comes from the purest depths of your own self:

> *And whoever shall say a word against the Son of man it shall be forgiven him; but to him that speaks injuriously against the Holy Spirit it shall not be forgiven. But when they bring you before the synagogues and rulers and the authorities, be not careful how or what ye shall answer, or what ye shall say; for the Holy Spirit shall teach you in the hour itself what should be said. (Luke 12:10-12)*

THE FALSE PROPHET

The writings of the Pentateuch also seek to justify the extermination of entire communities and to teach people not only to hold a grudge against their enemies for their entire lives but also maintaining that ill will against their descendants for several generations. Whereas Jesus, without hesitation, strongly rebuked his disciples when they spoke of destroying some Samaritans who had refused to welcome them in their town:

> *They didn't receive him, because he was traveling with his face set towards Jerusalem. When his disciples, James and John, saw this, they said, 'Lord, do you want us to command fire to come down from the sky, and destroy them, just as Elijah did?' But he turned and rebuked them, 'You don't know of what kind of spirit you are. For the Son of Man didn't come to destroy men's lives, but to save them. (Luke 9:53-56)*

Nevertheless, still there will be those who continue to cling to the Moses of the Pentateuch, arguing that in chapter 5 of the Gospel of Matthew it is written that, "Until the heaven and the earth pass away, one iota or one tittle shall in no wise pass from the law till all come to pass"; however, they fail to see that in the same chapter, verse after verse, Jesus was criticizing the mundane nature of the laws stated in the books of the Pentateuch, which on many occasions, more than being simply imperfect, they were plain wrong and vicious.

If the Pentateuch had acknowledged that its laws were the work of man, Jesus words against it would not be as consequential. The problem here is that the books of Pentateuch alleged that most of its laws came straight from God, a claim that does not stand a chance when Jesus starts to prove how ungodly those laws are.

Coming back to the phrase from chapter 5 in the Gospel of Matthew, it is often pertinent to compare the different gospels to shed some light on issues that, at first glance, seem not to make sense. For instance, a similar phrase is said in Luke 16:17-18 when Jesus was rebuking the Pharisees, who saw themselves as protectors of the law; but in this case he made the statement with a very different tone, implying that it was impossible to change the law because of man's stubbornness. The true intention behind those verses is shown when Jesus, after having made the remark, intentionally contradicts one of the laws of the Pentateuch regarding the subject of divorce: "...But it is easier that the heaven and the earth should pass away than that one tittle of the law should fail. Everyone who puts away his wife and marries another commits adultery; and every one that marries one put away from a husband commits adultery." With such words, Jesus opposes Deuteronomy 24:1, where marriage is taken lightly and divorce is embraced with joy to satisfy man's self-centered disposition and insensitive attitude towards women.

That is, right at that very moment, when Jesus is saying that, "it is easier that the heaven and the earth should pass away than that one tittle of the law should fail", he is also demonstrating that the law of the Pentateuch is flawed, implying its mundane nature and illustrating men's reluctance to change their traditions even when they are wrong.

Interestingly enough, close to the end of the Book of Revelation, after the first and second beast have been defeated, it is written, "And I saw a new heaven and a new earth; for the first heaven and the first earth had passed away, and the sea exists no more" (Revelation 21:1). This phrase would have looked normal had it not been for the latter part that says "the sea exists no more." Why would the writer waste valuable ink and papyrus on something so trivial as the sea, especially within such an extraordinary statement regarding a new heaven and a new earth? Such is the case because in this instance the sea carries a hidden meaning, which can also be understood after reading Luke 16:17-18 and its remark concerning

THE FALSE PROPHET

heaven and earth in relation to the law. The sea represents the law of the Pentateuch, and Revelation 21:1 implies that after defeating the false prophet, under the new ideology, the law will "exist no more."

Bearing that in mind, the sea and its symbolic meaning is the same for Revelation 8:8-12, where a third part of the sea became blood after the second angel sounded his trumpet. What happened to the sea in that earlier section of the writing is part of a larger context in which, similarly, the fresh waters and the celestial bodies were also damaged. When the third angel sounded his trumpet, the rivers and fountains of waters became bitter and many men died because of this. Then the fourth angel sounded his trumpet and a third part of the moon, a third part of the sun and a third part of the stars were darkened. Hence, the second, third and fourth trumpets, which correspond to the sea, the fresh waters and the celestial bodies, respectively, were warnings implying that one-third of each of them had been altered in a certain way.

Knowing what has already been explained concerning the meaning of the number 666 and the identity of the false prophet, and taking into account the words of Revelation 21:1, where the phrase "the sea exists no more" refers to the Pentateuch—known in antiquity as the Law—, it can be inferred that the fountains of water from the third trumpet and the celestial bodies from the fourth trumpet refer to the other two sections of the Old Testament since in ancient times people used to arrange those books in three groups: The Law, the Writings and the Prophets. The warnings given concerning the damaged done to one-third of them is alluding to the idea that a portion of those ancient writings had been adulterated.

Still, despite the countless instances in which some of those writings promote unrighteous behavior in the name of God, people will try to deny that the hand of man has introduced ignorance and deception into them, always affirming that all of them were inspired by the Creator in their entirety.

WHEN THE THUNDERS SPEAK

Very often, no matter how spiritual we think we are, our mundane heart is too proud to discard those sensational stories that we have come to love so deeply, even when our own conscience tells us that our devotion to such writings is nothing more than vanity. On other occasions, our conscience has become so atrophied from inactivity and indifference, that we commit the great error of claiming that some writings must be believed without questioning, supposedly because they cannot be understood by man. But blind faith is just spiritual blindness, and what appear to be an unbreakable determination to support empty doctrines is merely our own fear of being wrong. Such a fear is born of ignorance and confusion, but true understanding is always able to tell apart light from darkness, wheat from tares, and righteous men from false prophets.

The teachings of Jesus embody an invaluable source of wisdom that allows the spirit of man to emerge even in the most adverse circumstances; a kind of wisdom that is capable of bringing forth goodness even in the most wicked human being. However, that cannot be achieved unless we learn how to exercise our own discernment in order to rise above certain doctrines that have been holding us back by professing admiration for imperfection.

The disagreement between Jesus' teachings and the Pentateuch is immense and it is in plain sight for all to see. We must be humble enough to admit that the two paths lead in opposite directions, and we have to be wise enough in order to choose the right one.

Jesus not only caused one tittle of the law to fail, he overthrew the law almost completely. His actions and words confirm this.

In addition to his actions and the teachings that were imparted to men in an open manner, he also gave us parables whose real meaning alluded to the danger of merging his doctrine with the ones that preceded him. When reading the Gospels, it is essential to take into consideration the circumstances under which they were written, which were marked by an intense religious intolerance that

THE FALSE PROPHET

boasted of destroying every person or writing that rejected the doctrine of the priests and their idols. They vilified, humiliated and destroyed anyone who dared to throw away the traditions and laws of the past; nevertheless, the Gospels found a way to do it by using parables in which Jesus insinuated that his teachings were not compatible with the doctrines of the past:

> *No one sews a patch of new cloth on an old garment: otherwise its new filling-up takes from the old, and there is a worse rent. And no one puts new wine into old skins; otherwise the wine bursts the skins, and the wine is poured out, and the skins will be destroyed; but new wine is to be put into new skins. (Mark 2:21-22)*

While in the Gospel of Luke was written: "But Jesus said to him, 'Leave the dead to bury their own dead, but you go and announce the Kingdom of God.' Another also said, 'I want to follow you, Lord, but first allow me to bid farewell to those who are at my house.' But Jesus said to him, 'No one, having put his hand to the plow, and looking back, is fit for the Kingdom of God'" (Luke 9:60-62).

It is clear that the Pentateuch contradicts Jesus in many instances, but if there is still some hesitation concerning which one of those two paths should be followed, an answer can be found in the hidden meaning behind the following verses:

> *And there appeared to them Elias with Moses, and they were talking with Jesus. And Peter answering says to Jesus, Rabbi, it is good that we should be here; and let us make three tabernacles, for thee one, and for Moses one, and for Elias one. For he knew not what he should say, for they were filled with fear. And there came a cloud overshadowing them, and there came a voice out of the cloud, this is my beloved Son: hear him. And suddenly having looked around, they no longer saw any one, but Jesus alone with themselves. (Mark 9:4-8)*

10

RETAKING THE PATH

What is truth?

"What is truth?" Pilate asked him, given that Jesus had told him a moment before that he came into the world to bear witness to the truth, and that only those who are of the truth listen to his voice.

At that point in time, the writing does not mention what was the reply to the question raised by Pilate because it had already been answered by Jesus again and again through his actions and teachings. What is truth? His testimony: that the spirit is not a slave of tradition; that by saying he had "overcome the world," he shows the way for others to do it as well; that man's destiny is not to remain weak but to liberate his spirit and become a son of the Creator; that compassion and forgiveness are non-negotiable; that going halfway is the same as not going at all; that the Giver of Life has never demanded bloody sacrifices, but justice, mercy, humbleness and self-control; that creation is one and is sustained by brotherhood; that the spirit does not cling to anything but the truth.

There was great confusion during the first century, and, to a certain degree, there still is today. Numerous sects emerged, and they all claimed to be bearers of the truth, but, in reality, most of them were blinded by the banality of their traditions and the hardness of their hearts. When the unrighteous are drowning in a sea of ignorance, they use hypocrisy to stay afloat, but they never make it to the land. In this way, many people claimed that establishing cruel laws was just, memorizing vainglorious stories was wise, and performing superficial rituals made them clean; but the testimony of Jesus against them was a categorical declaration that brought sanity to the mind and life to the soul.

However, even if the truth were to be revealed a thousand times, the mundane man will always value and respect his customs more than the sincerity of his own conscience because tradition is an old man of flesh and bones that he can see and touch. Certainly, traditions are valuable for shaping the identity of the people, considering that they were established by our ancestors since very ancient times, but the truth is more ancient than time, wiser than our ancestors and much more real than our identities.

The purpose of creation

What an amazing universe! All these wonders and mysteries. The true nature of a creature is not measured according to its current condition but to the potential it carries within it.

Trying to understand the purpose of life without being willing to put to the test the most basic concepts of reality is like trying to learn how to swim in a small puddle of water; you may see and touch the water, but you can only learn how to swim by submerging yourself in its depth. There are things that cannot be learned from others but just through yourself. This is why the worthy disciple is the one who becomes his own teacher. Man must seek and experiment; he must put the mind to the test, the body under his control and the spirit in action.

Creation is the exceptional opportunity to experience existence; even so, man has found ways to breathe, eat and laugh without realizing that he is alive. With so much illusory entertainment coming from the outside, man has lost the capacity to look inward and reflect.

RETAKING THE PATH

To experience his existence, man requires free will, without which he is nothing but inconsequential matter in motion; but having true free will also means coming into this world without a preconceived idea, without any prior knowledge. Being born in ignorance is an enormous but necessary obstacle that, when it is overcome, reveals the existence in all its splendor, and an extraordinary reality is discovered.

Understanding is the ability to discern a reality that is composed of qualities that go beyond the sensory boundaries of the body or the emotional weaknesses of the mind. Man needs to train himself to see what his eyes cannot perceive, for it is impossible to enter a place he cannot find, and it is nonviable to dwell with someone he cannot understand. First, he must develop the ability to comprehend where the flesh ends and the spirit begins. Unless he makes a fresh start with a new pair of eyes that do not distort the image of reality, he will continue to miss out on the most sublime elements of creation.

We must finally rise to the occasion and face the great distorter that stands between us and the door that leads to reality. If we do not have the vision to see through him, our vitality will be consumed little by little in the midst of illusion; trying to go around him will not take us anywhere near the door either. The only way to do it is by walking forward knowing that he vanishes when confronted with serenity.

The distorter

Depending on the angle you are looking at it from, his appearance may seem like a disturbing nightmare or like a pleasant dream, but in both cases, his obscure purpose stays the same, enslaving the mind of man and alienating him from reality. He uses people's weaknesses to blur the truth and lock them up in a world of triviality that is a labyrinth where being lost becomes man's most fulfilling goal.

WHEN THE THUNDERS SPEAK

Distorting reality is his power, and he uses it with such dexterity that only a few men manage to escape his trap. Out in the open, the distorter is very popular among the multitudes, while others, who seem to repudiate him, have quietly built an altar to him inside their minds. We are not talking about the false prophet, whose identity has been revealed in the previous chapter. The distorter is rather what man has come to know as sin.

Sin has been misunderstood for generations and continues to be an obscure concept that causes endless debates, some of which end in tragedies when the intolerance of the ritualists unleashes its violence against the slaves of sin, never realizing that by doing so, they too fall into its trap. While atheists, on the other hand, welcome sin by claiming that there is nothing wrong as long as they are not harming others, but fail to understand that the damage is done to themselves when they allow their perception of reality to be distorted by their weaknesses and addictions.

In order to overcome sin, it is necessary to understand it. There is no man who can catch a poisonous snake without first studying the animal to such an extent that would allow him to predict its movements. Once he learns how to approach the creature and where to hold it to immobilize it, there are no snakes left in the swamp that could harm him. The confusion lies in the very definition of sin. If we do not really understand what it is and what it causes, much less will we be able to understand how and why it must be overcome. Sin is the great distorter of reality, which by means of the ego makes men want to live in a small box created by their carnal and emotional weaknesses, instead of living in the vast reality of existence. Sin is not a definite number of actions that have been forbidden because someone decided to impose on us a set of rules; rather, sin is an obstacle that stuns or intoxicates the mind of man, clouding his vision and preventing him from reaching understanding.

RETAKING THE PATH

As a result of not being able to explain what sin really is, many still think that no sin is being committed as long as there is no evil intention involved. In this way, they try to justify all their addictions and aberrations and, on some occasions, for instance, have even established cults that revere sex, believing that self-indulgence is freedom and depravity is wisdom. In a state of permanent intoxication, they eventually die without realizing they ever existed and miss entirely the reality that was always in front of them. All this just because we have not been able to explain what sin is.

Those who supposedly know the truth yell, "Do not sin!" but when others ask them why, they simply say, "because it is written." And without further clarification, they dare to say that it is beyond our comprehension. Due to such a poor explanation, many people decide to end their search for the truth or join other doctrines that are equally wrong. Since the experts do not provide credible answers, the rest choose to follow other paths, this time not seeking the truth, but in search of the ideology that is the most convenient for the flesh; a doctrine that would be already aligned with their current mental state and would allow or even promote weaknesses that instead should be overcome. What benefit is there in a doctrine that speaks much of love but promotes the debauchery of the flesh? Or another that speaks of submission to God but encourages hatred and intolerance towards their brothers?

Due to the lack of understanding in these matters, man ends up twisting everything for his own convenience. If man is instructed not to lay in bed with his neighbor's wife, he then looks for the floor to do so. Sin is not a simple rule; it is everything that enslaves your body and your mind. In order to understand it, it is necessary to comprehend how infirmities distort reality and destroy your character.

WHEN THE THUNDERS SPEAK

Sin is living in ignorance without any understanding of what is truly real. Man has a great intellect, but regardless of how many books he reads, he will still live in ignorance until he acknowledges that most of his thoughts are flawed in every sense. In an unconscious manner, his intellect has become biased towards the type of behaviors that stimulate the mind and body in an instant, while it refuses, without even trying, those things that in the beginning require much discipline and patience. In the midst of his blindness, his mind is not so dissimilar to the inexperienced mind of a baby, the difference being that the little boy has only the vice of sucking his thumb, while men, even those who believe themselves to be righteous, have more vices than all the fingers of their hands; men are obsessed with money, sex, the palate, emotional aberration, vainglory and being constantly entertained. And if one of those things is removed from their mouths, men feel miserable, and their souls drown in tears.

When man is finally able to understand that sin is the great distorter of reality and that by corrupting the mind, it keeps him entertained in states of daze or vain pleasure, then he will learn that avoiding the act is not enough to defeat it. He must also overcome it in the battle that is always fought in the mind; only by changing his current nature can man defeat the distorter. Sin makes reality irrelevant, reducing the experience of existence to a tiny world whose limits are defined by the extremely short-sighted ego. Yet, when we are able to set foot in the reality that reconcile all contradictions, the great distorter is not great at all; in fact, he is miniscule.

Corruption of the mind

Man came into existence to achieve clarity in his vision, but his own mind has imprisoned him, his carnal weaknesses have become heavy chains, and traditions turned out to be the prison guards. Will this be his ultimate fate, or will he ever realize that the guards are under his command and that the stiffness of the prison bars is an illusion that, with a small stroke of reason, would collapse into pieces?

A healthy mind is a mind in order that understands the difference between need and desire, between soundness of mind and custom, between what is just and what is legally permitted. If we are not able to make these distinctions, we should label ourselves as mentally ill. Yet, such a term tends to be used just when describing those people who do not behave the same way as the majority. But what if most men were also suffering from some level of mental illness? Certainly, it would be impossible to notice it because it would be the new normal. Is the ordinary behavior of men sane, or is it simply widespread madness that has become common among us?

Whenever men bow down to the distorter, they offer in sacrifice a portion of their mental integrity, whose deterioration gradually worsens the perception of reality until it reaches a point where facts become relative and the urge to satisfy vain desires become an absolute need. Man's mind, far from being in order, has forgotten that truth is found in simplicity. Reality is one, but the perception of it varies according to any particular habit and every single addiction; the more man clings to his weaknesses, the closer he gets to madness.

The mind of the ordinary man is not so different from that of the deranged one; both their minds are obsessed with vain things, just to different degrees. The vices of the wicked are evident, while the vices of the ordinary man are kept secret, but both their minds are corrupt. The wicked man can neither control his thoughts nor his actions; while the ordinary man, although he controls his actions, can seldom control his thoughts.

Man is born with an empty mind that can be easily corrupted by his carnal condition when he lacks the drive to understand his own self. The adulteration of the mind is not a particularity of criminals but an innate condition of the flesh and an outcome of man's ignorance that must be faced and overcome by every being endowed with free will. We all have a degree of ignorance that must be eradicated, but he who does not know how to find flaws in himself will never see any true virtue either. Both the young and the old are blind, both the rich and the poor. It is evident that the immoral are blind, but often even the judges are. The former believe there has never been a need for eyes. The latter think there is nothing left to see. Anyone who is convinced that there is nothing else to learn is proudly wearing a blindfold in front of the most stunning sunrise.

There is corruption in every man, but in each one, it can be eradicated. Chaos can be found in every mind. The only difference is the illusion that nourishes it. For the rich, the corruption of the mind is fed by the entertaining ecstasy derived from material things and the false sense of happiness they provide; yet, it will never be profitable nor sustainable trying to find everlasting happiness in finite things. While the minds of the poor degrade if anxiety is allowed to steal their peace; thus, let it be known that peace of mind is the most valuable asset a man can have and should not be left unguarded nor sold for scraps. As for the young, their minds are suppressed by vanity and procrastination; if only they knew how much those who have found the truth wish they had found it much earlier, for the bliss and beauty of the truth cannot be matched by the shallow pleasures of unconscious living. While for men of age, very often their stubbornness of clinging to their presumed acquired knowledge makes their discernment immature and their minds unable to fully grow; a knowledgeable man should know that his many years of experience amounts to nothing if he is unable to experience the present in its entirety.

RETAKING THE PATH

As for the immoral, how is their mind different from everyone else? Any small unrestrained vice can lead men to mischief: desperation makes people steal from their brothers; men deceive their neighbors for money; feelings are destroyed to protect the ego; excessive privileges reign over fairness so that a few men can preserve a distinguished place among many, and the mind is taken hostage by the desires of the flesh and does not even know it. Everyone feeds their vices with a different type of food, but they all breathe the same polluted air of false perception. Self-destruction has become a way of life, for every vice does not only have the ability to cause harm to others, but it also always has the peculiarity of wrecking the mind of whoever harbors such vice.

Even the ordinary little distortions of the mind result in its corruption. Both permanent stress and boredom are the direct result of a distorted mind. Boredom is nothing more than the inability to perceive the fascinating nature of one's existence. Nowadays, endless collections of vain entertainment can be found everywhere by everyone, but the true self is nowhere to be found. Man continues to stray away from himself, and when he is alone in silence, instead of finding calmness, he only finds desperation and a terrifying sense of emptiness. In this day and age, any ordinary man has more amusements at the tip of his fingers than any king from ancient times ever dreamt of; however, you may have an army of buffoons at your disposal just to make you laugh, but if your own soul cannot make you smile from within, your mind will be doomed to a dull existence that becomes unbearable every time a moment of silence asks you to look inward.

By means of an everlasting frenetic search for illusory and vain entertainments, we pretend to hide the great void that just the spirit can permanently fill. And yet, we still insist on killing time when in fact time is killing us.

WHEN THE THUNDERS SPEAK

The mind is conditioned by habit. Such conditioning does not allow us to judge with sincerity and keeps us in absolute ignorance concerning our own existence. The most obvious example is the different notions concerning violent behavior. If a young man grows up surrounded by cruel acts that are applauded, by the time he reaches adulthood, he will hardly see them as violence, except if he ventures into deep reflection.

That is the case with terrorists training children, but it can also happen to any normal soldier, a child with a careless upbringing or to anyone who repeats a long-held tradition without question. There are numerous examples that illustrate how people become accustomed to violence, but there is one particular case that is thought-provoking and contentious: animal cruelty as entertainment or for personal pleasure. This is so controversial because it challenges long-held traditions and habits. In such cases, man not only gets used to violence, but he also celebrates it, gets excited about it and, in some instances, even gets addicted to it.

The minds of many feel amused by bloody acts that they even get to call "sports", from dog and cockfighting to hunting for pleasure and bullfights. In the latter, for instance, the bull is first surrounded by the *banderilleros* and the bullfighter who chases the animal as if harassing the weak was an extravaganza. Then, two *picadores* riding their horses start stabbing the bull's neck with their lances to weaken its muscles until the animal becomes incapable of fully lifting its head. Afterwards, the *banderilleros* come forward to pierce the victim with their sticks (*banderillas*), which are shaped like harpoons so that after penetrating the flesh, they hang and swing every time the animal moves. And finally, in the third act, the bullfighter shows up walking like a sensual dancer before stabbing the animal with a sword (*estoque*) that is long enough to cause a fatal blow to internal organs. As twisted as it is, the spectators then start applauding and smiling in approval of the not-so-great feat, while the commentator can be heard in the background saying: "What a spectacular night. What a magnificent show!"

How is it possible that the same event is able to bring so much pleasure to some people, but it causes the exact opposite reaction in others? How many other things do we enjoy doing that are actually not enjoyable at all?

Although human beings are the creatures with the greatest intellect on the planet, in many cases, our species has become the least rational. Even wild animals show more self-control than man, who has surrendered all his power to drugs, addictive toxic foods and meaningless entertainment that rusts the mind. Instead of feeling satisfied with his life of debaucheries and vain pleasures, man must recognize that such weaknesses, besides being the cause of innumerable diseases, have also clouded his reason and buried his spirit. The intellect, one of man's greatest strengths, has become his Achilles' heel. Man uses his powerful mind just to find the most effective way to satisfy the excessive and distorted desires of his body, or to conceal his emotional weaknesses, rather than rising above them.

Both too much entertainment and extreme labor have taken the mind to a point where it feels lifeless in the absence of external stimuli, and, like a child, it runs from one place to another and despises silence unless it is already half asleep.

To restore the vision, the mind does not need to be filled with overwhelming and endless readings. It only needs to be cleansed through self-control and cleared by reflection. It needs to slow down just enough so that it is able to see itself.

Whenever you reach a dead end and cannot see the fascinating reality that exists beyond all the noise and circus lights, train yourself by visualizing your mind in the darkest, farthest and emptiest place you can imagine, and realize how your presence alone would quietly but surely fill that entire space. There is nothing there but your own presence, and yet it is fulfilling. Bring that genuine feeling back to the actual place you are in, and become aware of the fact that you are much more than just your physical senses.

Two dictators, lust and gluttony

After millennia of innumerable losses and sufferings caused by plunder and violence, many nations have come to realize that all-out conflicts are a lavish display of injustice that brings great misery to too many people for the benefit of a few ruling mercenaries; however, when the nature of ignorance is not understood in its entirety, irrationality never disappears. It simply morphs into something else, and men went from abusing their neighbors to abusing their own bodies and banishing their own souls. Men were able to break free from their cruel oppressors only to find themselves governed by lust and gluttony, two dictators that seized power by deceiving their followers into thinking that happiness depended on one single criterion: humanity's ability to stretch the pleasures of the flesh beyond the limits of good judgment and call it sanity.

Because we have failed to define in a proper way the inherent harm caused by lust and gluttony, men embrace them with pride and happily allow their minds to be ruled by such weaknesses, becoming mere subjects of those who decreed that mental lucidity has no use and that self-control is a rebel. The human race was endowed with an impressive mind, but a powerful mind with no self-control can only lead to great obsessions, which in turn lead to a mental unrest most people do not even realize they have. Such a condition is marked by a never-ending anticipation of the next treat for the physical senses; a repetitive emotional state that puts the mind in a position in which it has neither enough time to grow nor tranquility to see clearly.

Can any soul find peace if the mind is always in a heightened state of alert for all the wrong reasons? Can the spirit become aware of its own strength when man persistently chooses to be weak? The soul seems to be free, but it is kept on a short leash by lust and gluttony, and whenever it tries to move in any direction, all of a sudden it is pulled back by one of them. The greater the obsession, the shorter the leash, but this fact is often ignored because a widespread obsession is always seen as the norm.

Here lies the great power of these two infirmities, for the word obsession is a very subjective term, yet it is an obstacle with serious consequences for the human mind. Man cannot have it both ways; the mind is either lucid or weak. Discipline and moderation bring about clarity, while addictions bring man down to his knees, and procrastination makes him forget how strong he is.

For as long as it can be remembered, gluttony and lust have been threatening the mental and spiritual integrity of man, but in recent times their dominion has reached every corner of the known world because what used to be a luxury of kings and aristocrats is now in the plates and hearts of everyone. Even among the souls that are exploited and oppressed again and again, the little amount of spare time that has been rightly earned is wrongly spent. Man is still far from understanding that what he calls "spare time" is in fact the most valuable time he has, and instead of embracing an attitude that edifies, he is fine with devoting himself to a repetitive behavior that destroys, voraciously doing the same thing again and again as if it were something new to him.

Man has figured clever means to harness the power of nature in unimaginable ways thanks to his unparalleled determination, but he is always hesitant to harness his own vitality. Industrial advances are used for the wrong purpose, and technology is often too much for a negligent mind that only seeks to keep its fleshly desires alive at every instant. In earlier times, man could not rest because he was concerned with his survival, but now that he has survived, he will not rest until he sees his own demise.

WHEN THE THUNDERS SPEAK

Unconsciously, being a victim of his own mental abilities, man has become so obsessed with the pleasures of the flesh that he has come to see them as needs. And if he were asked to choose between breathing and his dearest carnal desire, he would almost suffocate before making his choice. In that manner, the line between need and desire has been blurred to such an extent that even nature is perplexed at the widespread debauchery that rules over what is supposed to be the most intelligent creature on the planet.

Man becomes a slave of a mechanism that he does not even understand. It does not matter how eloquent someone may appear to be; his elegant words are often a reflection of his weaknesses more than a demonstration of his intellect. He may be clever when convincing others to accept his opinion; however, reason is not determined by the number of people who support a certain argument but by the sturdiness of the truth that sustains it.

Sensory abilities are necessary for physical survival, but abusing them in an uncontrolled manner and for an indefinite time only leads to chaos within the body, confusion in the mind and despair in the soul. Nevertheless, lust and gluttony are now daily routines that have become idols for humanity. Countless uncontrolled thoughts run through the mind day and night. Although they seem harmless, the frequency with which they occur is sufficient to prevent anyone from reaching the level of lucidity that is needed to find pleasure in existence itself.

One day a young man visited a town square for the first time, and immediately he noticed the presence of an attractive woman that caught his attention. They started a conversation, which later became a beautiful relationship. But such a pleasing experience made him come back to the town square every day for the sole purpose of meeting other women to repeat the same feeling.

Even after becoming much older and trained in many trades, he continued visiting the town square year after year for the same reason as before. He knew then that even though he had a place to sleep and break bread, his home was the town square, and his food was something else.

One morning, the now old man woke up only to find out that his body could not move any longer. He was not able to hear either, except for a voice that was coming from within and which he could not distinguish if it was from himself or someone else. Terrified, he asked for help, but he could only hear the voice, and just the voice could hear him.

"It is time to leave. If you show me the way, I'll take you home," the voice said to him. But the old man was puzzled by this request and not sure where he wanted to go given that his body was not responding. After giving it much thought, the old man said he wanted to go to that place full of peace and beauty that his mother used to talk about. "Just show me the path, and I'll take you there," the voice replied.

Still, the old man did not have any idea how to get there. He had just realized that, despite his old age and vast experience, his soul was incapable of depicting anything other than the town square. Even worse, he could only perceive this from his narrow perspective, which merely consisted of his romantic encounters and unstable relationships. His uncontrollable mind kept wanting to go back to those old times of conquests, even though the town square had much more to offer, such as the song of birds, the laughter of children playing, the inspiring sight of the youth and the elders interacting with each other, a beautiful sunset and many other wonders that an indifferent mind is not able to see, nor a worn-out perception able to appreciate.

The old man's mind could not see beyond his old desires, and such was the only world he could understand. The voice said to him, "the realm your soul knows is the exact place where your body is lying down right now, and there is where you want to be, for no one can truly desire something he does not know. You do not need me."

Afraid of seeing himself dissolve into nothingness, the old man started complaining about how useless the voice was. But the voice replied, "I know only what you have taught me. You do not know the path because you have never taken me there, and you have never taken me there because you never cared to explore. Perhaps you did not have to go farther than the town square, just deeper."

The voice continued, "Several things I learned from you: you cannot dwell in a place where you do not want to be, and you cannot actually see or touch a kingdom that you do not comprehend. Even if there were a way to take you there, you would greatly despise that place because you are not ready for it. For you, the concepts that sustain that other realm are absurd and bizarre, while those things that you consider necessary and beautiful are useless there."

Many people end up liking the razor-thin surface layer more than the dense core; they peel the fruit just to eat the skin and throw away the rest. This is so because the physical senses can only perceive the appearance of existence, not its essence. A scuba diver loves the vast world that lies beneath the ocean's surface because he is able to see it clearly, while anyone who lacks the proper equipment and training can only see a very distorted image of that reality or nothing at all.

When a man is not able to control his thoughts, he is blinded by his desires and fails to see the great wonders that surround him as well as the small things that gradually lead him to the truth. But this great tragedy should in no way be blamed on others, but rather it is due to the lack of self-control of the person in whom lust manifests. Thus, the only effective and sincere way to overcome this weakness is by training the mind not to lose control over such desires and not through methods that hide the infirmity by putting burdens on someone else. When the hull of a ship breaks, the solution is not to dry up the sea to prevent water from entering but to repair the ship.

It is something extraordinary when a relationship is not centered on sex, but on trust, mutual help and the sharing of experiences; and even more delightful when the relationship, besides being the source of procreation, becomes the ideal place for raising a child. Marriage is a place for learning, where daily practice teaches the couple the true value of sacrifice. However, when the ego is the master of their will, the relationship ends up being conditioned by every whim of their sexual desires. Marriage is not a place to sanctify the lack of restraint but a sanctuary for the mind, which protects itself from perversion by practicing moderation and prudence.

Very often, man cannot get past puberty, a stage in which he sometimes remains stuck until reaching old age. If a young man patiently takes his time to discover the nakedness of his beloved lady, why doesn't he make a similar effort to discover the mysteries of existence? Life is much more than a particular group of chemical reactions, and it is not wise to let the mind stall because of an ordinary desire whose repetition takes you to the same place where you started. When thoughts cannot be controlled, the only option left for the conscience is to wane away, and its absence inevitably leaves the door wide open for ignorance to take over. Such ignorance is a corpse's way of pretending to be alive. Acting by mere instinct is no different than behaving as a pre-programmed machine since instinct itself is a negation of consciousness, without which there is no free will. Still, lust continues to have a firm grip on those who do not value, or simply are not aware of, the nature of lucidity.

The other dictator, gluttony, just like the previous one, has also convinced his followers that his ephemeral benevolence is the ultimate accomplishment. His subjects not only have to surrender their minds to his will, but they also have to sacrifice their health in his name, obeying and applauding every command of the dictator with devotion. Logic and reason have been thrown to the ground, the principles of the spirit have been neglected, life has been disrespected, and even with the body itself we have been irreverent. When man allows himself to be ruled by gluttony, he enters a state of conformity that brutalizes him. In such conditions, his blurred version of happiness can only be achieved through the palate. In this way, man forces his bowels to receive everything that his palate dictates, not by necessity but by the perversion of the senses.

At its core, the palate represents a formidable skill by which the body senses what kind of nutrients it needs at a certain moment, but uncontrolled habits and the excessive use of flavors have distorted its function. With each bite, unconsciously many have come to think that the purpose of life is to satisfy the sense of taste; hence, without even realizing it, their search for happiness sadly ends at the table.

We live in a highly illogical and irrational society. Willingly, man consumes poison every single day, renouncing both mental clarity and good quality of life while welcoming dozens of diseases that overwhelm the understanding of even the most reputable doctors. In such a manner, dictator gluttony has ordered a genocide of his own followers, which is carried out in a slow but certain way until everyone has taken their last bite. Everyone has been invited; some do not last long, others may make it through the night, but none of the guests survive the false sense of happiness that prevents them from feeling alive until the next feast.

Everything has been allowed for the sake of gluttony, even being indifferent to immoral actions that are committed simply to satisfy our vices. Cruelty is part of the menu, but an endless appetite always numbs the heart and blinds all reason.

When sitting at the dining table, it is more convenient to invite reason, which always brings along self-control, moderation,

RETAKING THE PATH

humility, mercy and respect; on the other hand, if you let addiction take over your seat, you will also have to make room for its four ravaging children: debauchery, arrogance, indifference and impiety.

Even when an addiction is not harmful to the physical body, it is still highly detrimental to mental soundness, given that vices create a psychological dependence that conditions happiness to a particular habit, which is a clear distortion of reality. An addict believes that he is making use of his free will, but he is deceiving himself because there has never been more than one option for him; the only path an addict can see is the one that his vices command.

Gluttony and lust will have you running in circles as if there were nothing else to contemplate; hence, you have to be strong enough to uproot them both but also wise enough to understand that a lesser pleasure can only be overcome by embracing a superior one. For if a ditch remains unfilled, the same man who dug it could easily fall in it when it is dark. If a large crowd of men were to overthrow a cruel ruler just to leave the throne vacant, sooner or later, the same ruler would return to take it back with an even more destructive rage.

When moderation is practiced with grace, it never becomes a burden because self-control does not leave you empty-handed, but it grants you what you have always lacked. It is not about taking away the only thing you believe you have but about revealing everything that is actually yours. For the desires of the flesh are like a luxurious blindfold made of the most expensive silk. It might feel incredibly soft to the touch and give you a sense of comfort, but just by ridding yourself of it will you be able to see.

Thus, when you are ready for the challenge, remember to do it not as a punishment but, on the contrary, because you have an eager desire to clear your mind in order to discover the most genuine freedom that any being could experience in the flesh. And if you ever feel vulnerable, a slight smile on your face will certainly remind you how strong you are and how insignificant and illusory your old demons have always been.

Comfortable dungeon of mammon

Regardless of how glamorous and impressive a castle may appear to be, it is nothing more than polished stones and sculpted pieces of wood before the eyes of eternity.

Vanity calls herself queen but kneels before money and deception, and it would crawl and beg, or bite if necessary, for the most superficial recognition; while the greatness of simplicity lies in the fact that it humbles itself in front everyone, but it does not feel humiliated by anything. Despite its disposition to serve, simplicity only prostrates itself at the feet of the truth.

On many occasions, the writings about Jesus warn against trusting in riches, and they use specific parables to illustrate how difficult it is for the rich to see beyond the material world. Yet, it is habitual for people to ignore Jesus' words while, at the same time, claiming to be his most fervent followers. It is disheartening that many of his teachings are neglected even by a large number of preachers who, instead of praising the virtues of simplicity and humility, engage in an outrageous race to accumulate wealth, encouraging others to do the same.

Why are the writings about Jesus so emphatic against the accumulation of wealth? What could be so dangerous about something that appears to be so harmless? Why do we have such an inclination to soften his words and give another interpretation to his teachings? The subject is not that complicated, but our fears and weaknesses make it impossible to understand.

For a man to be fully aware of the greater reality that surrounds him, his vision has to be stronger than his fear of losing his possessions. When he believes that his happiness depends on the things he owns, this lie becomes his own degraded reality where genuine beauty is beyond his understanding, and true power is no longer within his reach. However, the wealthy are not the only ones who fall into the trap of mammon. Those who have a strong desire to become rich, as well as those who are not at peace with themselves because of the things they lack, are too burdened to comprehend or even enjoy that which was given to them at no cost.

Preparing for tomorrow is part of a prudent and natural behavior, but allowing the probabilities of the future to always steal the certainties of the present is unfortunate for the soul. Most of us claim that we want to accumulate just enough to cover our needs, but when we get there, what we once saw as abundance is suddenly too little; soon we become terrified of losing any of those things we have obtained over time, even when we do not need them. The more material goods we have, the more we cling to the false notion that life would be unbearable without those possessions.

Survival instinct is governed by fear, while the spirit is driven by freedom. Thus, in order to experience the fullness of existence, it is necessary to overcome the anxiety that is always present in the mind due to the possibility of either losing material things or not being able to acquire them in the first place. Fear causes man to work tirelessly all day long to buy himself a dungeon with golden bars in which he incarcerates his mind. Each decision and each thought end up being tied to his beloved dungeon. All despite the fact that man never had the need to kneel before riches since he has always owned something that not even the most powerful conglomerate could afford or manipulate: his precious spirit.

The spirit begins where tradition ends

The truth cries out to the man of science and says to him, "Go and do your experimentation and tell me if my logic fails: What is more real, vanity or simplicity?" While to him who adores the desires of the flesh, the truth says: "Go ahead and get intoxicated until your soul is depleted and your mind loses its splendor, and if somehow you are able to recover some level of clarity, ask yourself: What is more fulfilling and lasting, the chaos of debauchery or the order of self-control?" And to him who claims to know what virtue is, the truth asks: "Where will you find me, in fascinating stories or humble teachings, in the tradition of the past or the reflection of the present?"

Breaking the chains of ill-founded traditions is just the beginning. The face of the false prophet has been revealed thanks to a brilliant clue that was written in the Book of Revelation around two thousand years ago. An ancient testimony that will shake our entire belief system and challenge our understanding; a legacy that is determined to restore the path that leads to the truth and clear the name of the Creator from all the mundane misconstructions that have been used to crush the spirit of men.

The second beast has been exposed, and it has been shown how, by simple means, the number 666 confirms his identity beyond any doubt. Now it is up to us to use this knowledge to perfect our ways instead of settling for behaviors that we thought were justified. To understand the great power and influence that this mysterious figure continues to exert on men, we must simply examine how his commands were used to decide who would live or die for millennia and how his laws and acts were able to shape the mindset of today to the extent that perverse attitudes disguised as morality take precedence even over kindness, humility and self-control. Well-intentioned instructions, as originally conceived, were blatantly buried under layers and layers of mundane and cruel machinations.

They tried to disfigure the essence of that which created us. They wanted our Father to be a murderer so we could also be murderers, but the true children of Judah testified against those who claimed to be the keepers of their forefathers' traditions. The writings that were corrupted by priests and kings could not corrupt the hearts of the humble and meek.

Regardless of the circumstances, true peace can only be found within the most genuine freedom, which is freedom from vices and fear, but the road begins with trials, self-discipline and resolve because a weak spirit is not a spirit at all. As man walks through the desert, the strength he needs to continue the expedition is found in the understanding that there is immense pleasure in self-control when it is empowered by contemplation and driven by clarity of mind. Very often, what people perceive as strength in another person is simply the ability of that individual to find joy in something that the majority has not grown to understand; thus, becoming strong is about learning to see the beauties that his old weaknesses did not allow him to appreciate. Still, in the same path where he finds awe, he will also find consternation; awe because his eyes will be opened, and consternation because he will long for others to see.

The most important revelation is the one that man will discover when something inside him begins to cry out for him to let it sprout. Then the past will die out, and the present will be born for the first time. Reality will at last be revealed before its own children, whose eyes will no longer be deceived by the illusion of materialism and superficiality; the ego that was previously hidden in the character of man will be seen as an obnoxious stain that ruins the garment and diverts his attention. The habits of the past will be despised by man, who will abandon hypocrisy and finally be able to live in peace with his own reflection.

What at the beginning of the journey seemed like a sacrifice is indeed a great pleasure. The degree of man's understanding has no limits, and no one is born to remain in ignorance nor to settle for half-truths. Man has come to exist to grow indefinitely while there are truths to learn and weaknesses to overcome. However, he needs to make sure that what is growing is in fact the spirit and not the ego, which also increases easily with vain knowledge from endless readings.

Man has come to prefer darkness because light reveals his deformities. Only when he has the faith and determination to accept that these deformities can be healed will he understand that light is needed to do so, and he will not be afraid or despise it any longer.

He who wishes to find the truth must stop time and learn to be aware of what he is. Such a thing does not require much reading but deep reflection. The greatness of existence and the immense value of his being can only be understood when in the middle of his reflection, he realizes that he is not a university degree nor a bank account nor a name nor a culture nor a failure. When he visualizes himself after all those things have been removed and carefully discerns what remains, he will know what he is made of and will be aware of the great value that lies within him and within every being in his surroundings. At that moment, he will start contemplating reality without those distortions that degrade its quality. It will then become evident that true pleasure is not derived from expensive toys or ordinary circumstances but from being grateful for existence itself.

Calamities can break a tough man, and temptations and addictions can tie up a strong one, but anyone who is at peace with himself will not remain broken for long nor will he allow himself to be constrained by illusory ropes. Adversities will always be seen as a dead end for someone eager to give up, whereas for an inquisitive mind, the eventualities of life are occasions to train harder and meditate in a more pure way. Life is an opportunity, not a tragedy, and its circumstances are challenges, not a punishment.

The past does not condemn anyone but the present; it is not the committed acts from the past that ruin man but rather the ignorance at which he has arrived because of them. The distortions created by

RETAKING THE PATH

his vices accumulate over time and impair his ability to see the most virtuous dimensions of existence.

The ignorance begotten by pernicious habits is like an immense wall that a man built by stacking stone upon stone throughout all the days of his life. Suppose one day he decides to take down the wall because he realized that the vibrant view behind it is much more glorious than the wall itself. In that case, he will also need to understand that the wall that took years to build cannot be torn down with one blow; instead, he will have to take it down stone by stone, day by day, in a subtle but persistent way. If he is hesitant, he will end up removing a stone one day and putting it back in the wall the very next day, repeating this futile effort for the rest of his life, always wondering why he can't see past the wall.

Discernment is knowing that you cannot have both the wall and the magnificent view behind it; surrendering your ego is accepting that the wall you built must be taken down; determination is taking down the wall stone by stone, and vision is what you get when you are done.

The time is always now, and the crucial place is wherever you are. No external event will ever match or outlast that which originates from within you. Life is a mystery, and if you look carefully, even in the confines of your mind, you will find wonders that are impossible to describe. You do not have to look for great signs in the sky to break up the monotony of your life, and your faith should not rest on a physical event but on a spiritual one.

Many questions have the potential to devour the most brilliant minds of entire nations, but just one question is really worth answering within the individuality of man. If it is true that perfection can never be achieved, then such a statement simply means that there is an infinite number of ways of making yourself better. If this is so, having no intention of improving your character is the most disheartening and illogical way of wasting the opportunity of a lifetime.

Take heed and do it now. Grab every opportunity as if it were your only chance to liberate your mind, for procrastination is a powerful demon that can only be overcome with determination. When sound reasoning is turned into good habits, good habits turn into virtues. Virtues will then become the nature of man and he will learn to live according to those principles, not for the purpose of receiving a reward in a distant future but because he derives great pleasure from them in the present moment. On that day, there will be no unrighteous man who can turn him away from the truth, nor false prophets who can hold hostage his discernment.

It was necessary to reveal the true identity of the beast in order to escape the current stagnation and free ourselves from deception. Despite the overwhelming evidence, many will continue to defend the false prophet's indefensible behavior and instructions, while others will accept the evidence but will get stuck, for a while, in the mud of contentious disputes. Yet, if one advances with introspection, not with the intention of judging others but of improving oneself, it will become evident that by clinging to our traditions, we have come to use an old and dirty dress to clothe an unblemished teaching that never needed clothing. By having done so, for millennia, we have buried the truth, but the letter of Revelation was written to vindicate it.

Many will try to use the words of this book in an incendiary way to create controversy and more division. Still, the ultimate purpose of the truth is always to bring peace by eradicating the contradictions that afflict the mind and burden the soul. Discernment must be our religion and conflict our only enemy.

ABOUT THE AUTHOR

Melvin E. Paredes-Forzani was born and raised in Santo Domingo, Dominican Republic. He pursued his undergraduate studies in the United States, where he received a Bachelor of Science in Mechanical Engineering from Utah State University. Later, at the same university, he completed a Master of Science in Applied Economics, with a specialization in Regional Economic Development.

Paredes-Forzani has worked as a mechanical design engineer, production manager, diplomat and policy advisor. He started his professional career in Utah, United States, but later moved back to the Dominican Republic and then to Canada, where he now lives with his wife and three sons.

The author describes himself as a person who admires simplicity and finds greatness in the little things of life. He considers that, regardless of one's career path or personal circumstances, the primary purpose of all individuals should be to find within themselves the truth that moves their existence, and that such a search must not be subordinated to their habits, culture or the worries of daily life.

www.ingramcontent.com/pod-product-compliance
Lightning Source LLC
Chambersburg PA
CBHW030907080526

44589CB00010B/186